B.C.

JESUS AS TEACHER

Books by

H. B. SHARMAN

JESUS AS TEACHER
RECORDS OF THE LIFE OF JESUS
SON OF MAN AND KINGDOM OF GOD
STUDIES IN THE RECORDS
PAUL AS EXPERIENT
Harper and Brothers

TEACHING OF JESUS ABOUT THE FUTURE
University of Chicago Press

JESUS IN THE RECORDS
Association Press

JESUS AS TEACHER

By

Henry Burton Sharman Ph D

HARPER & BROTHERS PUBLISHERS

New York and London

JESUS AS TEACHER

Printed in the United States of America

D-I

CONTENTS

PROLOGUE

PROLOGUE † † † †

For one whose major interest, relative to Jesus, has its base in his thinking and teaching, many portions of the records that have reached us concerning Jesus make no contribution. They lack content of teaching, and they provide nothing toward the outline structure of the history.

Because we have four different records about the events of the life of Jesus, many accounts duplicate what is to be had elsewhere. Often the similarities are so close that the parallels do not have any separate or distinctive value for one whose concern is with the main historical movements and the substance of the thought.

Sayings of Jesus are reported as frequently as five or more times in widely differing contexts and sometimes in strikingly divergent forms. It becomes the task of the serious student to endeavor to determine the occasion or occasions of the saying and to press back through its several reported forms to that which may be regarded as most nearly its original cast.

Some of the makers of our books about Jesus have used notable freedom in their distribution of the source material that was at their disposal. Any study of the book of Matthew which takes account of the other books will make that fact evident to the observant reader. In that freedom—obviously exercised by an author who had literary sources but no immediate knowledge—may be inherent some justification for such transpositions of material as are ventured upon by the maker of *Jesus As Teacher*.

Major contemporary national hopes of the people of Jesus have left their imprint deeply upon the traditions of his life and teaching. Segregation of these messianic elements has been effected here not only because, on critical grounds, their nature seems alien to the mind of Jesus but also because they supply vividly the background of his activity and teaching.

When that which was resident and implicit in the personal religion of Jesus made its way into the Hellenistic world, it apparently became explicit through the creation of another type of biographical representation. While appeal may not be confidently made to the record of John for the accurate phrasing of the sayings of Jesus, nor may all of the elements in the self-consciousness there portrayed be assuredly attributed to him (least of all certain forms of their expression), forthright dismissal ought not perhaps to be made of the philosophy and psychology of religion there sketched as being altogether out of harmony with the essential position of Jesus elsewhere depicted.

When the concern is to discover the foundations for the judgments exercised in the construction of *Jesus As Teacher*, or when the interest ranges beyond the limits of the teaching of Jesus, reference may be made to *Records of the Life of Jesus*—where the complete phenomena of the canonical traditions about Jesus are set forth with freedom from surmises or theories but in such form as to provide the bases for independent conclusions as to both teachings and events.

BOOK I

THE RECORD OF MATTHEW MARK AND LUKE

BOOK I: THE RECORD OF MT-MK-LK

STATEMENTS ABOUT ORIGINS

Chapter I: Statements About Origins

§1 Origin of the Records
§2 Birth of Jesus at Bethlehem
§3 The Dedication at Jerusalem
§4 The Return to Nazareth
§5 The Youth of Jesus
§6 Jesus As Student
§7 Development of Jesus

§1 Origin of the Records

FORASMUCH as many have taken in hand to draw up a narrative concerning those matters which have been fulfilled among us, even as they delivered them unto us, which from the beginning were eyewitnesses and ministers of the word, it seemed good to me also, having traced the course of all things accurately from the first, to write unto thee an orderly account, most excellent Theophilus; so that thou mightest know the certainty concerning the things wherein thou wast instructed.

§2 Birth of Jesus at Bethlehem

In the days of Herod, king of Judæa, it came to pass that there went out a decree from Cæsar Augustus, that all the world should be enrolled. This was the first enrolment made when Quirinius was governor of Syria. And all went to enrol themselves, every one to his own city.

And Joseph also went up from Galilee, out of the city of Nazareth, into Judæa, to the city of David, which is called Bethlehem, because he was of the house and family of David; to enrol himself with Mary, who was great with child.

And it came to pass, while they were there, the days were fulfilled that Mary should be delivered. And she brought forth her firstborn son; and she wrapped him in swaddling clothes, and laid him in a manger, because there was no room for them in the inn.

§3 The Dedication at Jerusalem

And when eight days were fulfilled for circumcising him, his name was called JESUS.
And when the days of their purification according to the law of Moses were fulfilled, they brought Jesus up to Jerusalem, to present him to the Lord (as it is written in the law of the Lord, Every male that openeth the womb shall be called holy to the Lord), and to offer a sacrifice according to that which is said in the law of the Lord, A pair of turtledoves, or two young pigeons.

§4 The Return to Nazareth

And when they had accomplished all things that were according to the law of the Lord, they returned into Galilee, to their own city Nazareth.

§5 The Youth of Jesus

And the child Jesus grew, and waxed strong, becoming full of wisdom: and the grace of God was upon him.

§6 Jesus as Student

And the parents of Jesus went every year to Jerusalem at the feast of the passover. And when Jesus was twelve years old, they went up after the custom of the feast. And when they had fulfilled the days, as they were returning, the boy Jesus tarried behind in Jerusalem. And his parents knew it not; but supposing him to be in the company, they went a day's journey. And they sought for him among their kinsfolk and acquaintance: and when they found him not, they returned to Jerusalem, seeking for him.

And it came to pass, after three days they found him in the temple, sitting in the midst of the teachers, both hearing them, and asking them questions: and all that heard him were amazed at his understanding and his answers.

And when they saw him, they were astonished: and his mother said unto him, Son, why hast thou thus dealt with us? behold, thy father and I sought thee sorrowing. And Jesus said unto them, How is it that ye sought me? wist ye not that I must be in my Father's house? And they understood not the saying which he spake unto them.

§7 Development of Jesus

And Jesus went down with his parents, and came to Nazareth; and he was subject unto them: and his mother kept all these things in her heart.

And Jesus advanced in wisdom and stature, and in favour with God and men.

ACTIVITY OF JOHN AND ITS RELATION TO JESUS † † †

Chapter II: Activity of John and Its Relation to Jesus

§8 Statement of the Work of John

Now in the fifteenth year of the reign of Tiberius Cæsar, Pontius Pilate being governor of Judæa, and Herod being tetrarch of Galilee, and his brother Philip tetrarch of the region of Ituræa and Trachonitis, and Lysanias tetrarch of Abilene, in the high-priesthood of Annas and Caiaphas,
the word of God came unto John the son of Zacharias in the wilderness of Judæa. And he came into all the region round about Jordan, preaching the baptism of repentance unto remission of sins.
¶ It is written in the book of the words of Isaiah the prophet,

The voice of one crying in the wilderness,
Make ye ready the way of the Lord,
Make his paths straight.
Every valley shall be filled,
And every mountain and hill shall be brought low;
And the crooked shall become straight,
And the rough ways smooth;
And all flesh shall see the salvation of God.

¶ Now John himself had his raiment of camel's hair, and a leathern girdle about his loins; and his food was locusts and wild honey.
Then went out unto him all they of Jerusalem, and all the country of Judæa, and all the region round about Jordan; and they were baptized of him in the river Jordan, confessing their sins.
¶ But when John saw many of the Pharisees and Sad-

ducees coming to his baptism, he said unto them, Ye offspring of vipers, who warned you to flee from the wrath to come? Bring forth therefore fruits worthy of repentance, and begin not to say within yourselves, We have Abraham to our father: for I say unto you, that God is able of these stones to raise up children unto Abraham. And even now is the axe also laid unto the root of the trees: every tree therefore that bringeth not forth good fruit is hewn down, and cast into the fire.

¶ And all the people when they heard, and the publicans, justified God, being baptized with the baptism of John. But the Pharisees and the lawyers rejected for themselves the counsel of God, being not baptized of him.

¶ And the multitudes asked John, saying, What then must we do? And he answered and said unto them, He that hath two coats, let him impart to him that hath none; and he that hath food, let him do likewise.

And there came also publicans to be baptized, and they said unto him, Teacher, what must we do? And he said unto them, Extort no more than that which is appointed you.

And soldiers also asked him, saying, And we, what must we do? And he said unto them, Do violence to no man, neither exact anything wrongfully; and be content with your wages.

¶ And as the people were in expectation, and all men reasoned in their hearts concerning John, whether haply he were the Christ; John answered, saying unto them all,

I indeed baptize you with water; but there cometh he that is mightier than I, the latchet of whose shoes I am not worthy to unloose: he shall baptize you with fire: whose fan is in his hand, throughly to cleanse his threshing-floor, and to gather the wheat into his garner; but the chaff he will burn up with unquenchable fire.

¶ With many other exhortations therefore preached John good tidings unto the people; but Herod the tetrarch, being reproved by him for Herodias his brother's wife, and for all the evil things which Herod had done, added yet this above all, that he shut up John in prison.

§9 Baptism of Jesus by John

Now it came to pass, when all the people were baptized of John in the Jordan, that, Jesus also having been baptized, and praying, the heaven was opened, and the Spirit of God descended, as a dove, upon him. And a voice came out of heaven: Thou art my beloved Son; this day have I begotten thee.

§10 Withdrawal of Jesus to the Wilderness

And Jesus, full of the Spirit of God, returned from the Jordan, and was led by the Spirit in the wilderness during forty days, being tempted of the devil.

¶ And he led Jesus up, and shewed him all the kingdoms of the world in a moment of time. And the devil said unto him, To thee will I give all this authority, and the glory of them: if thou wilt worship before me, it shall all be thine. And Jesus answered and said unto him, It is written, Thou shalt worship the Lord thy God, and him only shalt thou serve.

¶ And he led Jesus to Jerusalem, and set him on the pinnacle of the temple, and said unto him, If thou art the Son of God, cast thyself down from hence: for it is written,

He shall give his angels charge concerning thee,
to guard thee:
And on their hands they shall bear thee up,
Lest haply thou dash thy foot against a stone.

And Jesus answering said unto him, It is said, Thou shalt not tempt the Lord thy God.

¶ And the devil said unto Jesus, If thou art the Son of God, command this stone that it become bread. And Jesus answered unto him, It is written, Man shall not live by bread alone.

BEGINNINGS OF THE PUBLIC ACTIVITY OF JESUS † † †

Chapter III: Beginnings of the Public Activity of Jesus

§11 General Statement of the Work of Jesus

AND Jesus returned in the power of the Spirit into Galilee: and a fame went out concerning him through all the region round about. And he taught in their synagogues, being glorified of all.

§12 Jesus Teaches at Nazareth

And Jesus came to Nazareth, where he had been brought up: and he entered, as his custom was, into the synagogue on the sabbath day, and stood up to read. And there was delivered unto him the book of the prophet Isaiah. And he opened the book, and found the place where it was written,

The Spirit of the Lord is upon me,
Because he anointed me to preach good tidings to the poor:
He hath sent me to proclaim release to the captives,
To set at liberty them that are bruised,
To proclaim the acceptable year of the Lord.

And he closed the book, and gave it back to the attendant, and sat down. And the eyes of all in the synagogue were fastened on him. And all bare him witness, and wondered at the words of grace which proceeded out of his mouth.

And they said, Is not this Joseph's son?

Jesus himself, when he began to teach, was about thirty years of age, being the son (as was supposed) of Joseph.

§13 Jesus Teaches at Capernaum

And Jesus came down to Capernaum, a city of Galilee. And straightway on the sabbath day he entered into the synagogue and taught. And they were astonished at his teaching: for he taught them as having authority, and not as the scribes.
And they were all amazed, insomuch that they questioned among themselves, saying, What is this? a new teaching!
And the report of him went out straightway everywhere into all the region of Galilee round about.

§14 Jesus and Mental Cases

And straightway, when Jesus was come out of the synagogue, he came into the house. And at even, when the sun did set, they brought unto Jesus them that were possessed with devils. And all the city was gathered together at the door. And he cast out many devils. And the devils came out crying and saying,
Ah! What have we to do with thee, thou Jesus of Nazareth, thou Son of the Most High God? Art thou come to torment us? Art thou come to destroy us? We know thee who thou art, the Holy One of God!
And rebuking them, Jesus suffered them not to speak, because they believed that he was the Christ.

§15 Jesus Teaches by the Lake

Now it came to pass, while the multitude pressed upon Jesus and heard the word of God, that he was standing by the lake of Gennesaret.
And he saw two boats standing by the lake: but the

fishermen had gone out of them, and were washing their nets. And he entered into one of the boats, which was Simon's, and asked him to put out a little from the land.
And he sat down and taught the multitudes out of the boat.

§16 Jesus Wins Fisherman Followers

And when Jesus had left speaking, he said unto Simon, Put out into the deep, and let down your nets for a draught. And Simon answered and said, Master, we toiled all night, and took nothing: but at thy word I will let down the nets.
And when they had this done, they inclosed a great multitude of fishes. And they beckoned unto their partners in the other boat, that they should come and help them. And they came, and filled both the boats.
And Simon was amazed at the draught of the fishes which they had taken; and so were also James and John, sons of Zebedee, which were partners with Simon.
But Simon Peter fell down at Jesus' knees, saying, Depart from me; for I am a sinful man, O Master.
And Jesus said unto Simon, Fear not; from henceforth thou shalt catch men.
And when they had brought their boats to land, they left all, and followed Jesus.

§17 Jesus Teaches Throughout Galilee

And in the morning, a great while before day, Jesus

rose up and went out, and departed into a desert place, and there prayed.
And Simon and they that were with him followed after him; and they found him, and say unto him, All are seeking thee.
And Jesus saith unto them, Let us go elsewhere into the next towns, that I may preach there also; for to this end came I forth.
And he went into their synagogues throughout all Galilee teaching.

DEVELOPMENT OF OPPOSITION TO JESUS † † † †

Chapter IV: Development of Opposition to Jesus

§18 Criticism of Free Forgiveness for Sin
§19 Criticism for Association with Sinners
§20 Criticism of Attitude Toward Fasting
§21 Criticism for Working on the Sabbath
§22 Culmination of Criticism of Jesus
§23 Attitude of Jesus Toward Criticism

§18 Criticism of Free Forgiveness for Sin

AND when Jesus entered again into Capernaum after some days, it was noised that he was in the house. And many were gathered together, so that there was no longer room for them, no, not even about the door.

And Jesus was teaching. And there were Pharisees and doctors of the law sitting by, which were come out of every village of Galilee and Judæa and Jerusalem.

And behold, men bring on a bed a man that was palsied: and they sought to bring him in, and to lay him before Jesus. And not finding by what way they might bring him in because of the multitude, they went up to the housetop, and let him down through the tiles with his couch into the midst before Jesus.

And Jesus seeing their faith saith unto the sick of the palsy, Son, thy sins are forgiven. But there were certain of the scribes sitting there, and reasoning in their hearts, Why doth this man thus speak? he blasphemeth: who can forgive sins but one, even God?

And straightway Jesus, perceiving in his spirit that they so reasoned within themselves, saith unto them, Why reason ye these things in your hearts? Man hath authority on earth to forgive sins.

Then Jesus saith to the sick of the palsy, I say unto thee, Arise, take up thy bed, and go unto thy house. And he arose, and departed to his house. But when the multitudes saw it, they glorified God, which had given such authority unto men.

§19 Criticism for Association with Sinners

And Jesus went forth again by the sea side; and all the multitude resorted unto him, and he taught them.
And as Jesus passed by, he saw Levi the son of Alphæus sitting at the place of toll, and he saith unto him, Follow me. And he arose and followed him. And it came to pass, that he was sitting at meat in his house, and many publicans and sinners sat down with Jesus and his disciples: for there were many, and they followed him.
And the scribes of the Pharisees, when they saw that Jesus was eating with the sinners and publicans, said unto his disciples, He eateth and drinketh with publicans and sinners. And when Jesus heard it, he saith unto them,
They that are whole have no need of a physician, but they that are sick: I came not to call the righteous, but sinners.
But go ye and learn what this meaneth, I desire mercy, and not sacrifice.

§20 Criticism of Attitude toward Fasting

And John's disciples and the Pharisees were fasting: and they come and say unto Jesus, Why do John's disciples and the disciples of the Pharisees fast, but thy disciples fast not?
And Jesus said unto them, Can the sons of the bride-chamber fast, while the bridegroom is with them? as long as they have the bridegroom with them, they cannot fast. But when the bridegroom shall be taken away from them, then will they fast.

§21 Criticism for Working on the Sabbath

And it came to pass, that Jesus was going on the sabbath day through the cornfields; and his disciples began, as they went, to pluck the ears of corn. And the Pharisees said unto him, Behold, why do they on the sabbath day that which is not lawful?
And Jesus said unto them, Did ye never read what David did, when he had need, and was an hungred, he, and they that were with him? How he entered into the house of God, and did eat the shewbread, which it is not lawful to eat save for the priests, and gave also to them that were with him?
Or have ye not read in the law, how that on the sabbath day the priests in the temple profane the sabbath, and are guiltless?
And Jesus said unto them, The sabbath was made for man, and not man for the sabbath: so that man is lord even of the sabbath.

§22 Culmination of Criticism of Jesus

And the Pharisees went out, and straightway with the Herodians took counsel against Jesus, how they might destroy him.

§23 Attitude of Jesus Toward Criticism

And Jesus spake also parables unto them:
No man rendeth a piece from a new garment and putteth it upon an old garment; else he will rend the new, and also the piece from the new will not agree with the old.
And no man putteth new wine into old wine-skins;

else the new wine will burst the skins, and itself will be spilled, and the skins will perish. But new wine must be put into fresh wine-skins.

And no man having drunk old wine desireth new: for he saith, The old is good.

DEFINITION OF STANDARDS OF RIGHTEOUSNESS BY JESUS † †

Chapter V: Definition of Standards of Righteousness by Jesus

§24 Widespread Fame of Jesus

AND Jesus with his disciples withdrew to the sea: and a great multitude from Galilee followed. And from Judæa, and from Jerusalem, and from Idumæa, and beyond Jordan, and about Tyre and Sidon, a great multitude, hearing what great things he did, came unto him.

And he spake to his disciples, that a little boat should wait on him because of the crowd, lest they should throng him: for as many as had plagues pressed upon him that they might touch him.

And the unclean spirits, whensoever they beheld him, fell down before him, and cried, saying, Thou art the Son of God. And he charged them much that they should not make him known.

§25 Appointment of Twelve Associates

And it came to pass in these days, that Jesus went out into the mountain to pray; and he continued all night in prayer to God.

And when it was day, he called his disciples: and he chose from them twelve, that they might be with him, and that he might send them forth: Simon, whom he also named Peter, and Andrew his brother; and James the son of Zebedee, and John the brother of James; and Philip and Bartholomew; and Matthew and Thomas; and James the son of Alphæus, and Simon which was called the Zealot; and Judas the son of James, and Judas Iscariot, which was the traitor.

§26 Discourse on Standards of Righteousness

And Jesus came down with the twelve, and stood on a level place. And a great multitude of his disciples, and a great number of the people from all Judæa and Jerusalem, and the sea coast of Tyre and Sidon, came to hear him.

¶ And Jesus lifted up his eyes on his disciples, and said:
Blessed are ye poor.
Blessed are ye that hunger.
Blessed are ye that weep.
Blessed are ye when men persecute you.
Ye are the salt of the earth.
Ye are the light of the world.

¶ Think not that I came to destroy the law or the prophets: I came not to destroy, but to fulfil. For I say unto you, that except your righteousness shall exceed the righteousness of the scribes and Pharisees, ye shall in no wise enter into the kingdom of God.

¶ Ye have heard that it was said to them of old time, Thou shalt not kill; and whosoever shall kill shall be in danger of the judgement: but I say unto you, that every one who is angry with his brother shall be in danger of the judgement.

If therefore thou art offering thy gift at the altar, and there rememberest that thy brother hath aught against thee, leave there thy gift before the altar, and go thy way, first be reconciled to thy brother, and then come and offer thy gift.

Blessed are the peacemakers: for they shall be called sons of God.

¶ Ye have heard that it was said, Thou shalt not commit adultery: but I say unto you, that every one that looketh on a woman to lust after her hath committed adultery with her already in his heart. And if thine eye causeth thee to stumble, pluck it out, and cast it from thee: for it is profitable for thee that one of thy members should perish, and not thy whole body. And if thy hand causeth thee to stumble, cut it off, and cast it from thee: for it is profitable for thee that one of thy members should perish, and not thy whole body.

Blessed are the pure in heart: for they shall see God.

¶ Again, ye have heard that it was said to them of old time, Thou shalt not forswear thyself, but shalt perform unto the Lord thine oaths: but I say unto you, Swear not at all; neither by the heaven, nor by the earth, nor by Jerusalem. Neither shalt thou swear by thy head. But let your speech be, Yea, yea; Nay, nay: and whatsoever is more than these is of evil.

¶ Ye have heard that it was said, An eye for an eye, and a tooth for a tooth: but I say unto you, Resist not evil: but whosoever smiteth thee on thy right cheek, turn to him the other also. And if any man would take away thy cloke, let him have thy coat also. And whosoever shall compel thee to go one mile, go with him twain.

Blessed are the meek: for they shall inherit the earth.

¶ Ye have heard that it was said, Thou shalt love thy neighbour, and hate thine enemy: but I say unto you, Love your enemies, do good to them that hate you, bless them that curse you, pray for them that despitefully use you.

If ye love them that love you, what thank have ye? for even sinners love those that love them. And if ye do good to them that do good to you, what thank have ye? for even sinners do the same.

Ye shall be sons of the Most High: for he is kind toward the unthankful and evil: he maketh his sun to rise on the evil and the good, and sendeth rain on the just and the unjust. Be ye merciful, even as your Father is merciful.

Blessed are the merciful: for they shall obtain mercy.

¶ Take heed that ye do not your righteousness before men, to be seen of them: else ye have no reward with your Father.

¶ When therefore thou doest alms, sound not a trumpet before thee, as the hypocrites do in the synagogues and in the streets, that they may have glory of men. Verily I say unto you, They have received their reward. But when thou doest alms, let not thy left hand know what thy right hand doeth: that thine alms may be in secret: and thy Father which seeth in secret shall recompense thee.

¶ And when ye pray, ye shall not be as the hypocrites: for they love to stand and pray in the synagogues and in the corners of the streets, that they may be seen of men. Verily I say unto you, They have received their reward. But thou, when thou prayest, enter into thine inner chamber, and having shut thy door, pray to thy Father which is in secret, and thy Father which seeth in secret shall recompense thee.

¶ Moreover when ye fast, be not, as the hypocrites, of a sad countenance: for they disfigure their faces, that they may be seen of men to fast. Verily I say unto you, They have received their reward. But thou, when thou fastest, anoint thy head, and wash thy face; that thou be not seen of men to fast, but of thy Father which is in secret: and thy Father, which seeth in secret, shall recompense thee.

¶ Why beholdest thou the mote that is in thy brother's eye, but considerest not the beam that is in thine own eye? Or how canst thou say to thy brother, Brother, let me cast out the mote that is in thine eye, when thou thyself beholdest not the beam that is in thine own eye? Thou hypocrite, cast out first the beam out of thine own eye, and then shalt thou see clearly to cast out the mote that is in thy brother's eye.

¶ All things therefore whatsoever ye would that men should do unto you, even so do ye also unto them.

¶ Not every one that saith unto me, Lord, Lord, shall enter into the kingdom of God; but he that doeth the will of my Father.

¶ By their fruits ye shall know them. For of thorns men do not gather figs, nor of a bramble bush gather they grapes. Every good tree bringeth forth good fruit; but the corrupt tree bringeth forth evil fruit. A good tree cannot bring forth evil fruit, neither can a corrupt tree bring forth good fruit. The good man out of the good treasure of his heart bringeth forth that which is good; and the evil man out of the evil treasure bringeth forth that which is evil. Therefore by their fruits ye shall know them.

¶ Every one therefore which heareth these words of mine, and doeth them, shall be likened unto a wise man, which built his house upon the rock: and the rain descended, and the floods came, and the winds blew, and beat upon that house; and it fell not: for it was founded upon the rock. And every one that heareth these words of mine, and doeth them not, shall be likened unto a foolish man, which built his house upon the sand: and the rain descended, and the floods came, and the winds blew, and smote upon that house; and it fell: and great was the fall thereof.

Enter ye in by the narrow gate: for wide is the gate, and broad is the way, that leadeth to destruction, and many be they that enter in thereby. For narrow is the gate, and straitened the way, that leadeth unto life, and few be they that find it.

¶ And it came to pass, when Jesus ended these words, the multitudes were astonished at his teaching: for he taught them as one having authority, and not as their scribes.

CONTEMPORARY OPINIONS ABOUT THE WORTH OF JESUS † †

Chapter VI: Contemporary Opinions About the Worth of Jesus

§27 Opinion of a Roman Centurion

AFTER Jesus had ended all his sayings in the ears of the people, he entered into Capernaum.

And a certain centurion, when he heard concerning Jesus, sent unto him elders of the Jews, asking him that he would save his boy. And they, when they came to Jesus, besought him earnestly, saying, He is worthy that thou shouldest do this for him: for he loveth our nation, and himself built us our synagogue.

And Jesus went with them. And when he was now not far from the house, the centurion sent friends to him, saying unto him, Sir, trouble not thyself: for I am not worthy that thou shouldest come under my roof: wherefore neither thought I myself worthy to come unto thee: but say the word. For I also am a man set under authority, having under myself soldiers: and I say to this one, Go, and he goeth; and to another, Come, and he cometh; and to my servant, Do this, and he doeth it.

And when Jesus heard these things, he marvelled at the centurion, and turned and said unto the multitude that followed him, I say unto you, I have not found so great faith, no, not in Israel.

§28 Opinion of John the Baptist

And the disciples of John told him of all these things. And John calling unto him two of his disciples sent them to Jesus, saying, Art thou he that cometh, or look we for another? And when the men were come unto Jesus, they said, John the Baptist hath sent us unto thee, saying, Art thou he that cometh, or look we for another?

And Jesus answered and said unto them, Go your way, and tell John what things ye have seen and heard. And blessed is he, whosoever shall find none occasion of stumbling in me.

And when the messengers of John were departed, Jesus began to say unto the multitudes concerning John, What went ye out into the wilderness to behold? a reed shaken with the wind? But what went ye out to see? a man clothed in soft raiment? Behold, they which are gorgeously apparelled, and live delicately, are in kings' courts. But what went ye out to see? a prophet? I say unto you, Among them that are born of women there is none greater than John: yet he that is but little in the kingdom of God is greater than John. He that hath ears to hear, let him hear.

From the days of John the Baptist until now the kingdom of God suffereth violence, and men of violence take it by force. For all the prophets and the law prophesied until John.

Whereunto then shall I liken the men of this generation, and to what are they like? They are like unto children that sit in the marketplace, and call one to another; which say, We piped unto you, and ye did not dance; we wailed, and ye did not weep. For John is come eating no bread nor drinking wine; and ye say, He hath a devil. I am come eating and drinking; and ye say, Behold, a gluttonous man, and a winebibber, a friend of publicans and sinners! And wisdom is justified of all her children.

§29 Opinion of a Sinner *vs* Opinion of a Pharisee

And one of the Pharisees desired Jesus that he would eat with him. And Jesus entered into the Pharisee's house, and sat down to meat. And behold, a woman which was in the city, a sinner; and when she knew that Jesus was sitting at meat in the Pharisee's house, she brought an alabaster cruse of ointment, and standing behind at his feet, weeping, she began to wet his feet with her tears, and wiped them with the hair of her head, and kissed his feet, and anointed them with the ointment.

Now when the Pharisee which had bidden Jesus saw it, he spake within himself, saying, This man, if he were a prophet, would have perceived who and what manner of woman this is which toucheth him, that she is a sinner.

And Jesus answering said unto him, Simon, I have somewhat to say unto thee. And he saith, Teacher, say on. Jesus said, A certain lender had two debtors: the one owed five hundred pence, and the other fifty. When they had not wherewith to pay, he forgave them both. Which of them therefore will love him most? Simon answered and said, He, I suppose, to whom he forgave the most. And Jesus said unto him, Thou hast rightly judged.

And turning to the woman, Jesus said unto Simon, Seest thou this woman? I entered into thine house; thou gavest me no water for my feet: but she hath wetted my feet with her tears, and wiped them with her hair. Thou gavest me no kiss: but she, since the time I came in, hath not ceased to kiss my feet. My head with oil thou didst not anoint: but she hath anointed my feet with ointment. Wherefore I say unto thee, Her sins, which are many, are forgiven; for she loved much.

And Jesus said unto the woman, Thy sins are forgiven. And they that sat at meat with him began to say within themselves, Who is this that even forgiveth sins? And he said unto the woman, Thy faith hath saved thee; go in peace.

§30 On a Tour in Galilee

And it came to pass soon afterwards, that Jesus went about through cities and villages, preaching and bringing the good tidings of the kingdom of God, and with him the twelve, and certain women which ministered unto them of their substance.

§31 Opinion of the Friends of Jesus

And Jesus cometh into a house. And the multitude cometh together again, so that they could not so much as eat bread. And when his friends heard it, they went out to lay hold on him: for they said, He is beside himself.

§32 Opinion of the Religious Leaders

And Jesus was casting out a devil. And it came to pass that when the devil was gone out the multitudes marvelled. And the scribes which came down from

Jerusalem said, He hath Beelzebub, and, By the prince of the devils casteth he out the devils.
And Jesus called them unto him, and said unto them, How can Satan cast out Satan? If a kingdom be divided against itself, that kingdom cannot stand but is brought to desolation. And every city or house divided against itself will not be able to stand, but falleth. And if Satan hath risen up against himself, and is divided, he cannot stand, but hath an end.
If I by Beelzebub cast out devils, by whom do your sons cast them out? Therefore shall they be your judges.
Verily I say unto you, Whosoever shall speak a word against me, it shall be forgiven him; but whosoever shall blaspheme against the Spirit of God, it shall not be forgiven him. This was because they said, He hath an unclean spirit.

THE MYSTERY OF THE KINGDOM OF GOD † † † † †

Chapter VII: The Mystery of the Kingdom of God

§33 Basis of Real Relationship to Jesus

AND there come his mother and his brethren; and, standing without, they sent unto Jesus, calling him. And a multitude was sitting about him; and they say unto him, Behold, thy mother and thy brethren without seek for thee. And he answereth them, and saith, Who is my mother and my brethren? Whosoever shall do the will of God, the same is my brother, and sister, and mother.

§34 Discourse on the Kingdom of God

And again Jesus began to teach by the sea side. And there is gathered unto him a very great multitude, so that he entered into a boat, and sat in the sea; and all the multitude were by the sea on the land. And he taught them many things in parables, and said unto them in his teaching:

¶ How shall we liken the kingdom of God? or in what parable shall we set it forth? It is like a grain of mustard seed, which, when it is sown upon the earth, though it be less than all the seeds that are upon the earth, yet when it is sown, groweth up, and becometh greater than all the herbs, and putteth out great branches; so that the birds of the heaven can lodge under the shadow thereof.

And again he said, Whereunto shall I liken the kingdom of God? It is like unto leaven, which a woman took and hid in three measures of meal, till it was all leavened.

And he said, Who hath ears to hear, let him hear.
¶Another parable set Jesus before them, saying, The kingdom of God is likened unto a man that sowed good seed in his field: but while men slept, his enemy came and sowed tares also among the wheat, and went away. But when the blade sprang up, and brought forth fruit, then appeared the tares also. And the servants of the householder came and said unto him, Sir, didst thou not sow good seed in thy field? whence then hath it tares? And he said unto them, An enemy hath done this. And the servants say unto him, Wilt thou then that we go and gather them up? But he saith, Nay; lest haply while ye gather up the tares, ye root up the wheat with them. Let both grow together.
If any man hath ears to hear, let him hear.
¶And Jesus said, So is the kingdom of God, as if a man should cast seed upon the earth; and should sleep and rise night and day, and the seed should spring up and grow, he knoweth not how. The earth beareth fruit of herself; first the blade, then the ear, then the full corn in the ear.
¶The kingdom of God is like unto a treasure hidden in the field; which a man found, and hid; and in his joy he goeth and selleth all that he hath, and buyeth that field.
Again, the kingdom of God is like unto a man that is a merchant seeking goodly pearls: and having found one pearl of great price, he went and sold all that he had, and bought it.
He that hath ears, let him hear.
¶And with many such parables spake Jesus the word

unto them, as they were able to hear it: and without a parable spake he not unto them.

¶And when Jesus was alone, the disciples came, and said unto him, Why speakest thou unto them in parables? And he said unto them, Unto you is given the mystery of the kingdom of God: but unto them that are without, all things are done in parables: that seeing they may see, and not perceive; and hearing they may hear, and not understand.

Give not that which is holy unto the dogs, neither cast your pearls before the swine, lest haply they trample them under their feet, and turn and rend you.

¶Then Jesus went into the house: and his disciples came unto him, saying, Explain unto us the parable of the tares of the field. And Jesus saith unto them, Know ye not this parable? and how shall ye know all the parables?

Take heed therefore how ye hear: for whosoever hath, to him shall be given; and whosoever hath not, from him shall be taken away even that which he thinketh he hath.

¶Hearken: Behold, the sower went forth to sow: and it came to pass, as he sowed, some seed fell by the way side, and the birds came and devoured it. And other fell on the rocky ground, where it had not much earth; and straightway it sprang up, because it had no deepness of earth: and when the sun was risen, it was scorched; and because it had no root, it withered away. And other fell among the thorns, and the thorns grew up, and choked it, and it yielded no fruit. And others fell into the good ground, and yielded fruit, growing up and increasing; and brought forth, thirtyfold, and sixtyfold, and a hundredfold.

¶And Jesus said unto them, Is the lamp brought to be put under the bushel, or under the bed, and not to be put on the stand? There is nothing hid, save that it should be manifested; neither was anything made secret, but that it should come to light.

¶And Jesus asked them, Have ye understood all these things? They say unto Jesus, Yea. And he said unto them, Therefore every scribe who hath been made a disciple to the kingdom of God is like unto a man that is a householder, which bringeth forth out of his treasure things new and old.

¶There is nothing covered up, that shall not be revealed: and hid, that shall not be known. What I tell you in the darkness, speak ye in the light: and what ye hear in the ear, proclaim upon the housetops. And I say unto you my friends, Be not afraid of them which kill the body, and after that have no more that they can do.

ACTIVITY ON TOURS OF JESUS AND DISCIPLES † † † †

Chapter VIII: Activity on Tours of Jesus and Disciples

§35 Fear *versus* Faith

Now it came to pass on one of those days, that Jesus entered into a boat, himself and his disciples; and he said unto them, Let us go over unto the other side of the lake. And leaving the multitude, they take him with them, even as he was, in the boat.
And there ariseth a great storm of wind, and the waves beat into the boat, insomuch that the boat was now filling. And he himself was in the stern, asleep on the cushion. And they awake him, and say unto him, Teacher, carest thou not that we perish?
And Jesus awoke, and said, Peace, be still. Why are ye fearful? have ye not yet faith?
And they came to the other side of the sea, into the country of the Gerasenes, which is over against Galilee.

§36 Jesus Teaches at Nazareth

And when Jesus had crossed over again in the boat unto the other side, he cometh into his own country; and his disciples follow him. And when the sabbath was come, he began to teach in the synagogue.
And many hearing him were astonished, saying, Whence hath this man these things? and, What is the wisdom that is given unto this man? Is not this the carpenter, the son of Mary, and brother of James, and Joses, and Judas, and Simon? and are not his sisters here with us?
And they were offended in Jesus. And Jesus said unto them, A prophet is not without honour, save in his

own country, and among his own kin, and in his own house.

§37 Jesus Teaches Throughout Galilee

And Jesus went about all the cities and the villages, teaching in their synagogues.

§38 Disciples Tour in Galilee

But when Jesus saw the multitudes, he saith unto his disciples, The harvest truly is plenteous, but the labourers are few. Pray ye therefore the Lord of the harvest, that he send forth labourers into his harvest.
And Jesus called unto him his twelve disciples, and began to send them forth by two and two. And he charged them that they should take nothing for their journey, save a staff only; no bread, no wallet, no money in their purse; for, said he, the labourer is worthy of his food.
And Jesus said unto them, Into whatsoever city or village ye shall enter, search out who in it is worthy. And as ye enter into the house, salute it. And if the house be worthy, let your peace come upon it. There abide till ye go forth, eating and drinking such things as they give. Go not from house to house.
He that receiveth you receiveth me, and he that receiveth me receiveth him that sent me.
And they went out, and preached that men should repent.

§39 Fate of John the Baptist

At that season Herod the tetrarch heard the report concerning Jesus, and said unto his servants, This is

John the Baptist, whom I beheaded; he is risen from the dead; and therefore do these powers work in him.
For Herod himself had sent forth and laid hold upon John, and bound him in prison. For John said unto Herod, It is not lawful for thee to have thy brother's wife. And for the sake of Herodias, his brother Philip's wife, Herod had sent and beheaded John in the prison.

§40 Report of Associates on Their Tour

And the twelve gather themselves together unto Jesus; and they told him all things, whatsoever they had done, and whatsoever they had taught. And he saith unto them, Come ye yourselves apart into a desert place, and rest a while. For there were many coming and going, and they had no leisure so much as to eat.

§41 Jesus Teaching in the Desert

And they went away in the boat to a desert place apart. And the people saw them going, and many knew them, and they ran there together on foot from all the cities, and outwent them.
And Jesus came forth and saw a great multitude, and he had compassion on them, because they were as sheep not having a shepherd: and he began to teach them many things.
And when the day was now far spent, Jesus constrained his disciples to enter into the boat, and to go before him unto the other side to Bethsaida, while he himself sendeth the multitude away. And after he had taken leave of them, he departed into the mountain to pray.

DEMAND BY PHARISEES FOR CONFORMITY AND CREDENTIALS † †

Chapter IX: Demand by Pharisees for Conformity and Credentials

§42 Concerning Traditions about Defilement

AND there are gathered together unto Jesus the Pharisees, and certain of the scribes, which had come from Jerusalem, and had seen that some of his disciples ate their bread with defiled, that is, unwashen, hands.

For the Pharisees, and all the Jews, except they wash their hands diligently, eat not, holding the tradition of the elders: and when they come from the market-place, except they wash themselves, they eat not: and many other things there be, which they have received to hold, washings of cups, and pots, and brasen vessels.

And the Pharisees and the scribes ask Jesus, Why walk not thy disciples according to the tradition of the elders, but eat their bread with defiled hands?

And Jesus said unto them, Well did Isaiah prophesy of you hypocrites, as it is written,

This people honoureth me with their lips,
But their heart is far from me.
But in vain do they worship me,
Teaching as their doctrines the precepts of men.

Ye leave the commandment of God, and hold fast the tradition of men.

And he said unto them, Full well do ye reject the commandment of God, that ye may keep your tradition. For Moses said, Honour thy father and thy mother; and, He that speaketh evil of father or mother, let him die the death: but ye say, If a man shall say to his father or his mother, That wherewith thou mightest have been profited by me is Corban, that is to say, Given to God; ye no longer suffer him to do aught for his father or his mother; making void the word of God by your tradition, which ye have delivered: and many such like things ye do.

¶ And Jesus called to him the multitude, and said unto them, Hear me all of you, and understand: To eat with unwashen hands defileth not the man. There is nothing from without the man, that going into him can defile him: but the things which proceed out of the man are those that defile the man.

¶ And when Jesus was entered into the house from the multitude, his disciples asked of him the parable. And he saith unto them, Are ye so without understanding also? Perceive ye not, that whatsoever from without goeth into the man, it cannot defile him; because it goeth not into his heart.

And he said, That which proceedeth out of the man, that defileth the man. For from within, out of the heart of men, evil thoughts proceed, fornications, thefts, murders, adulteries, covetings, wickednesses, deceit, lasciviousness, an evil eye, railing, pride, foolishness: all these evil things proceed from within, and defile the man.

¶ Then the disciples said unto Jesus, Knowest thou that the Pharisees were offended, when they heard that saying? But Jesus answered and said, Every plant which my Father planted not, shall be rooted up. Let them alone: they are blind guides. And if the blind guide the blind, both shall fall into a pit.

§43 Withdrawal toward Tyre and Sidon

And from thence Jesus arose, and went away into the borders of Tyre and Sidon. And he entered into a house, and would have no man know it: and he could not be hid.

§44 Return Journey through Decapolis

And again Jesus went out from the borders of Tyre and came through Sidon unto the sea of Galilee, through the midst of the borders of Decapolis.

§45 Pharisees Demand Signs from Jesus

And the Pharisees came forth, and began to question with Jesus, seeking of him a sign from heaven. And he sighed deeply in his spirit, and saith, Why doth this generation seek a sign? An evil and adulterous generation seeketh after a sign. Verily I say unto you, There shall no sign be given unto this generation. And he left them, and again entering into the boat departed to the other side.

§46 The Leaven of the Pharisees

And Jesus charged his disciples, saying, Take heed, beware of the leaven of the Pharisees and the leaven of Herod. And they reasoned one with another, saying, We have no bread.
Jesus perceiving it saith unto them, Why reason ye, because ye have no bread? do ye not yet perceive, neither understand? have ye your heart hardened? Having eyes, see ye not? and having ears, hear ye not?

And he said unto them, Do ye not yet understand? How is it that ye do not perceive that I spake not to you concerning bread? But beware of the leaven of the Pharisees and Sadducees. Then understood they how that he bade them not beware of the leaven of bread, but of the teaching of the Pharisees and Sadducees.

FORECASTS OF CONFLICT WITH THE JERUSALEM AUTHORITIES †

Chapter X: Forecasts of Conflict With the Jerusalem Authorities

§47 Opinion of Disciples about Jesus

AND Jesus went forth, and his disciples, into the villages of Cæsarea Philippi: and in the way he asked his disciples, saying unto them, Who do men say that I am? And they told him, saying, John the Baptist: and others, Elijah; but others, One of the prophets. And Jesus asked them, But who say ye that I am? Peter answereth and saith unto him, Thou art the Christ. Then charged Jesus the disciples that they should tell no man that he was the Christ.

§48 Jesus Forecasts Events at Jerusalem

From that time began Jesus to shew unto his disciples, how that he must go unto Jerusalem, and be rejected by the elders and chief priests and scribes, and be delivered up into the hands of men, and be condemned to death, and suffer many things, and be set at nought, and be killed.

And Peter took him, and began to rebuke him, saying, Be it far from thee, Master: this shall never be unto thee. But Jesus turned, and said unto Peter, Get thee behind me, Satan: thou mindest not the things of God, but the things of men.

§49 Some Costs of Discipleship

And Jesus called unto him the multitude with his disciples, and said unto them,

If any man would come after me, let him deny himself.

Whosoever would save his life shall lose it; but whosoever shall lose his life shall save it.
What is a man profited, if he gain the whole world, and lose or forfeit his own self?

§50 The Problem of Tribute Payment

And when they were come to Capernaum, they that received the half-shekel came to Peter, and said, Doth not your teacher pay the half-shekel? He saith, Yea.
And when he came into the house, Jesus spake first to him, saying, What thinkest thou, Simon? the kings of the earth, from whom do they receive toll or tribute? from their sons, or from strangers? And when he said, From strangers, Jesus said unto him, Therefore the sons are free.
But, lest we cause them to stumble, go thou to the sea, and cast a hook, and take up the fish that first cometh up: that take, and give unto them for me and thee.

§51 Teaching on Greatness

And when Jesus was in the house at Capernaum, he asked them, What were ye reasoning in the way? But they held their peace: for they had disputed one with another in the way, who was the greatest.
And Jesus sat down, and called the twelve; and he saith unto them, If any man would be first, he shall be last of all, and minister of all.
Salt is good: but if the salt have lost its saltness, wherewith will ye season it? Have salt in yourselves, and be at peace one with another.

§52 Teaching on Tolerance

John said unto Jesus, Teacher, we saw one casting out devils in thy name: and we forbade him, because he followed not with us. But Jesus said, Forbid him not: for there is no man which shall do a mighty work in my name, and be able quickly to speak evil of me. For he that is not against us is for us.

§53 Teaching on Forgiveness

And Jesus said unto his disciples, Take heed to yourselves: if thy brother sin, rebuke him; and if he repent, forgive him. And if he sin against thee seven times in the day, and seven times turn again to thee, saying, I repent; thou shalt forgive him.
Then came Peter, and said to Jesus, How oft shall my brother sin against me, Master, and I forgive him? until seven times? Jesus saith unto him, I say not unto thee, Until seven times; but, Until seventy times seven.

§54 Parable on Forgiveness

A certain king would make a reckoning with his servants. And when he had begun to reckon, one was brought unto him, which owed him ten thousand talents. But forasmuch as he had not wherewith to pay, his master commanded him to be sold, and his wife, and children, and all that he had, and payment to be made. The servant therefore fell down and worshipped him, saying, Master, have patience with me, and I will pay thee all. And the master of that servant, being moved with compassion, released him, and forgave him the debt.

But that servant went out, and found one of his fellow-servants, which owed him a hundred pence: and he laid hold on him, and took him by the throat, saying, Pay what thou owest. So his fellow-servant fell down and besought him, saying, Have patience with me, and I will pay thee. And he would not: but went and cast him into prison, till he should pay that which was due.

So when his fellow-servants saw what was done, they were exceeding sorry, and came and told unto their master all that was done. Then his master called him unto him, and saith to him, Thou wicked servant, I forgave thee all that debt, because thou besoughtest me: shouldest not thou also have had mercy on thy fellow-servant, even as I had mercy on thee?

DEPARTURE FROM GALILEE FOR JERUSALEM † † † †

Chapter XI: Departure from Galilee for Jerusalem

§55 General Statement of Journey
§56 Teaching on Tolerance
§57 Some Tests of Discipleship
§58 The Way of Eternal Life
§59 The Definition of Neighbour
§60 Many Things *vs* One Thing
§61 Elements of Prevailing Prayer
§62 Limitations of Exorcism
§63 Basis of Real Relationship to Jesus

§55 General Statement of Journey

AND it came to pass when Jesus had finished these words, he departed from Galilee. And multitudes come together unto him again; and, as he was wont, he taught them.
And when the days were well-nigh come that he should be received up, Jesus stedfastly set his face to go to Jerusalem.

§56 Teaching on Tolerance

And Jesus sent messengers before his face: and they went, and entered into a village of the Samaritans, to make ready for him. And they did not receive him, because his face was as though he were going to Jerusalem. And when his disciples James and John saw this, they said, Master, wilt thou that we bid fire to come down from heaven, and consume them? But Jesus turned, and rebuked them, and said, Ye know not what manner of spirit ye are of. And they went to another village.

§57 Some Tests of Discipleship

And as they went in the way, a certain man said unto Jesus, I will follow thee whithersoever thou goest. And Jesus said unto him, The foxes have holes, and the birds of the heaven have lodging-places; but I have not where to lay my head.
And Jesus said unto another, Follow me. But he said, Suffer me first to go and bury my father. But Jesus said

unto him, Leave the dead to bury their own dead. And another also said, I will follow thee, Master; but first suffer me to bid farewell to them that are at my house. But Jesus said unto him, No man, having put his hand to the plough, and looking back, is fit for the kingdom of God.

§58 The Way of Eternal Life

And behold, a certain lawyer stood up and questioned Jesus, saying, Teacher, what shall I do to inherit eternal life? And Jesus said unto him, What is written in the law? how readest thou? And he answering said, Thou shalt love the Lord thy God with all thy heart, and with all thy soul, and with all thy strength, and with all thy mind; and thy neighbour as thyself. And Jesus said unto him, Thou hast answered right: this do, and thou shalt live.

§59 The Definition of Neighbour

A certain lawyer said unto Jesus, Who is my neighbour? Jesus made answer and said,
A certain man was going down from Jerusalem to Jericho; and he fell among robbers, which both stripped him and beat him, and departed, leaving him half dead. And by chance a certain priest was going down that way: and when he saw him, he passed by on the other side. And in like manner a Levite also, when he came to the place, and saw him, passed by on the other side. But a certain Samaritan, as he journeyed, came where he was: and when he saw him, he was moved with compassion, and came to him, and bound up his

wounds, pouring on them oil and wine; and he set him on his own beast, and brought him to an inn, and took care of him. And on the morrow he took out some money, and gave it to the host, and said, Take care of him; and whatsoever thou spendest more, I, when I come back again, will repay thee.
Which of these three, thinkest thou, proved neighbour unto him that fell among the robbers? And he said, He that shewed mercy on him. And Jesus said unto him, Go, and do thou likewise.

§60 Many Things *vs* One Thing

Now as they went on their way, Jesus entered into a certain village: and a certain woman named Martha received him into her house. And she had a sister called Mary, which also sat at the Master's feet, and heard his word. But Martha was cumbered about much serving; and she came up to him, and said, Master, dost thou not care that my sister did leave me to serve alone? bid her therefore that she help me. But the Master answered and said unto her, Martha, Martha, thou art anxious and troubled about many things: but one thing is needful.

§61 Elements of Prevailing Prayer

And it came to pass, as Jesus was praying in a certain place, that when he ceased, one of his disciples said unto him, Master, teach us to pray, even as John also taught his disciples.
And Jesus said unto them, In praying use not vain repetitions, as the Gentiles do: for they think that they

shall be heard for their much speaking. Be not therefore like unto them: for God your Father knoweth what things ye have need of, before ye ask him.
After this manner therefore pray ye:
Father,
Hallowed be thy name.
Thy kingdom come.
Thy will be done, as in heaven, so on earth.
Give us day by day our daily bread.
And forgive us our sins; for we ourselves also forgive every one who has wronged us.
Therefore I say unto you, Whensoever ye stand praying, forgive, if ye have aught against any one; that your Father also may forgive you your trespasses.
And I say unto you, Ask, and it shall be given you; seek, and ye shall find; knock, and it shall be opened unto you. For every one that asketh receiveth; and he that seeketh findeth; and to him that knocketh it shall be opened.
And of which of you that is a father shall his son ask a loaf, and he give him a stone? or a fish, and he for a fish give him a serpent? Or if he shall ask an egg, will he give him a scorpion? If ye then, being evil, know how to give good gifts unto your children, how much more shall your Father give good things to them that ask him?
All things whatsoever ye pray and ask for, believe that ye have received them, and ye shall have them.

§62 Limitations of Exorcism

And Jesus was casting out a devil. And it came to pass,

when the devil was gone out, Jesus said,
The unclean spirit, when he is gone out of the man, passeth through waterless places, seeking rest, and findeth it not. Then he saith, I will return into my house whence I came out; and when he is come, he findeth it empty, swept, and garnished. Then goeth he, and taketh with himself seven other spirits more evil than himself, and they enter in and dwell there: and the last state of that man becometh worse than the first.

§63 Basis of Real Relationship to Jesus

And it came to pass, as Jesus said these things, a certain woman out of the multitude lifted up her voice, and said unto him, Blessed is the womb that bare thee, and the breasts which thou didst suck. But Jesus said, Yea rather, blessed are they that hear the word of God, and keep it.

DEEP FEELING AND DIRECT TEACHING † † † ⁘

Chapter XII: Deep Feeling and Direct Teaching

§64 Effects of the Mission of Jesus

IN THE mean time, when the many thousands of the multitude were gathered together, insomuch that they trode one upon another, Jesus began to say unto his disciples first of all,

Think ye that I am come to cast peace on the earth? I tell you, Nay; but rather division: for there shall be from henceforth five in one house divided, three against two, and two against three. They shall be divided, father against son, and son against father; mother against daughter, and daughter against her mother; mother in law against her daughter in law, and daughter in law against her mother in law. And a man's foes shall be they of his own household.

I came to cast fire upon the earth; and what will I, if it is already kindled? But I have a baptism to be baptized with; and how am I straitened till it be accomplished!

§65 The Signs of the Times

And Jesus said to the multitudes also, When ye see a cloud rising in the west, straightway ye say, There cometh a shower; and so it cometh to pass. And when ye see a south wind blowing, ye say, There will be a scorching heat; and it cometh to pass. Ye know how to interpret the face of the earth and the heaven; but how is it that ye cannot discern the signs of the times?

§66 Warnings of National Disaster

Now there were some present at that very season which told Jesus of the Galilæans, whose blood Pilate had mingled with their sacrifices. And he answered and said unto them,

Think ye that these Galilæans were sinners above all the Galilæans, because they have suffered these things? I tell you, Nay: but, except ye repent, ye shall all in like manner perish.

Or those eighteen, upon whom the tower in Siloam fell, and killed them, think ye that they were offenders above all the men that dwell in Jerusalem? I tell you, Nay: but, except ye repent, ye shall all likewise perish.

§67 Teaching About Reliance on Wealth

And one out of the multitude said unto Jesus, Teacher, bid my brother divide the inheritance with me. But Jesus said unto him, Man, who made me a judge or a divider over you?

And Jesus said unto them, Take heed, and keep yourselves from all covetousness: for a man's life consisteth not in the abundance of the things which he possesseth.

And Jesus spake a parable unto them, saying, The ground of a certain rich man brought forth plentifully: and he reasoned within himself, saying, What shall I do, because I have not where to bestow my fruits? And he said, This will I do: I will pull down my barns, and build greater; and there will I bestow all my corn and my goods. And I will say to my soul, Soul, thou hast much goods laid up for many years; take thine ease, eat, drink, be merry. But God said unto him, Thou foolish one, this night is thy soul required of thee; and the

things which thou hast prepared, whose shall they be? So is he that layeth up treasure for himself, and is not rich toward God.
Lay not up for yourselves treasures upon the earth, where moth and rust doth consume, and where thieves break through and steal: but lay up for yourselves treasure in heaven, where neither moth nor rust doth consume, and where thieves do not break through nor steal: for where thy treasure is, there will thy heart be also.

§68 Saying on Light and Darkness

And when the multitudes were gathering together unto Jesus, he began to say,
The lamp of thy body is thine eye: when thine eye is single, thy whole body also is full of light; but when it is evil, thy body also is full of darkness.
Look therefore whether the light that is in thee be not darkness. If the light that is in thee be darkness, how great is the darkness!

§69 Limits of the Kingdom of God

And Jesus went on his way through cities and villages, teaching, and journeying on unto Jerusalem.
And one said unto him, Master, are they few that be saved?
And Jesus said unto them, Strive to enter in by the narrow door: for many, I say unto you, shall seek to enter in, and shall not be able.
Ye shall see Abraham, and Isaac, and Jacob, and all the prophets, in the kingdom of God, and yourselves

cast forth without. And they shall come from the east and west, and from the north and south, and shall sit down in the kingdom of God.
And behold, there are last which shall be first, and there are first which shall be last.

§70 Forecast of his Death by Jesus

In that very hour there came certain Pharisees, saying to Jesus, Get thee out, and go hence: for Herod would fain kill thee. And he said unto them, Go and say to that fox, Behold, I must go on my way to-day and to-morrow, and the third day I am perfected: for it cannot be that a prophet perish out of Jerusalem.

§71 Teaching in Criticism of Anxiety

And Jesus said unto his disciples,
Be not anxious for your life, what ye shall eat, or what ye shall drink; nor yet for your body, what ye shall put on. Is not the life more than the food, and the body than the raiment?
Behold the birds of the heaven, that they sow not, neither do they reap, nor gather into barns; and God feedeth them. Are not ye of much more value than they?
And which of you by being anxious can add one cubit unto his stature?
And why are ye anxious concerning raiment? Consider the lilies of the field, how they grow; they toil not, neither do they spin: yet I say unto you, that even Solomon in all his glory was not arrayed like one of these. But if God doth so clothe the grass of the field

which to-day is, and to-morrow is cast into the oven, shall he not much more clothe you, O ye of little faith?
Be not therefore anxious, saying, What shall we eat? or, What shall we drink? or, Wherewithal shall we be clothed? For after all these things do the Gentiles seek.
Your Father knoweth that ye have need of all these things. Seek ye first his kingdom, and his righteousness; and all these things shall be added unto you.
Be not therefore anxious for the morrow: for the morrow will be anxious for itself. Sufficient unto the day is the evil thereof.

§72 Teachings at the Table of a Pharisee

And it came to pass that Jesus went into the house of one of the rulers of the Pharisees on a sabbath to eat bread.
And he spake a parable unto those which were bidden, when he marked how they chose out the chief seats; saying unto them,
When thou art bidden of any man to a marriage feast, sit not down in the chief seat; lest haply a more honourable man than thou be bidden of him, and he that bade thee and him shall come and say to thee, Give this man place. But when thou art bidden, go and sit down in the lowest place; that when he that hath bidden thee cometh, he may say to thee, Friend, go up higher. For every one that exalteth himself shall be humbled; and he that humbleth himself shall be exalted.

And he said to him also that had bidden him, When thou makest a dinner or a supper, call not thy friends, nor thy brethren, nor thy kinsmen, nor rich neighbours; lest haply they also bid thee again, and a recompense be made thee. But when thou makest a feast, bid the poor, the maimed, the lame, the blind: and thou shalt be blessed; because they have not wherewith to recompense thee.

§73 The Costs of Discipleship

Now there went with Jesus great multitudes: and he turned, and said unto them,
If any man cometh unto me, and hateth not his own father, and mother, and wife, and children, and brethren, and sisters, yea, and his own life also, he cannot be my disciple.
For which of you, desiring to build a tower, doth not first sit down and count the cost, whether he have wherewith to complete it? Lest haply, when he hath laid a foundation, and is not able to finish, all that behold begin to mock him, saying, This man began to build, and was not able to finish.
Or what king, as he goeth to encounter another king in war, will not sit down first and take counsel whether he is able with ten thousand to meet him that cometh against him with twenty thousand? Or else, while the other is yet a great way off, he sendeth an ambassage, and asketh conditions of peace.
So therefore whosoever he be of you that renounceth not all that he hath, he cannot be my disciple.
He that hath ears to hear, let him hear.

MANY TRUTHS TAUGHT IN PARABLES † † † †

Chapter XIII: Many Truths Taught in Parables

§74 Parables on the Worth of Sinners

NOW all the publicans and sinners were drawing near unto Jesus for to hear him. And both the Pharisees and the scribes murmured, saying, This man receiveth sinners, and eateth with them.

And Jesus spake unto them these parables, saying,

¶What man of you, having a hundred sheep, and having lost one of them, doth not leave the ninety and nine in the wilderness, and go after that which is lost, until he find it? And when he hath found it, he layeth it on his shoulders, rejoicing. And when he cometh home, he calleth together his friends and his neighbours, saying unto them, Rejoice with me, for I have found my sheep which was lost. I say unto you, that even so there shall be joy in heaven over one sinner that repenteth.

¶Or what woman having ten pieces of silver, if she lose one piece, doth not light a lamp, and sweep the house, and seek diligently until she find it? And when she hath found it, she calleth together her friends and neighbours, saying, Rejoice with me, for I have found the piece which I had lost. Even so, I say unto you, there is joy in the presence of the angels of God over one sinner that repenteth.

¶And he said, A certain man had two sons: and the younger of them said to his father, Father, give me the portion of thy substance that falleth to me. And he divided unto them his living. And not many days after the younger son gathered all together, and took his journey into a far country; and there he wasted his substance with riotous living. And when he had spent all, there arose a mighty famine in that country; and he began to be in want. And he went and joined himself to one of the citizens of that country; and he sent him into his fields to feed swine. And he would fain have been filled with the husks that the swine did eat: and no man gave unto him. But when he came to himself he said, How many hired servants of my father's have bread enough and to spare, and I perish here with hunger! I will arise and go to my father, and will say unto him, Father, I have sinned against heaven, and in thy sight: I am no more worthy to be called thy son: make me as one of thy hired servants. And he arose, and came to his father. But while he was yet afar off, his father saw him, and was moved with compassion, and ran, and fell on his neck, and kissed him. And the son said unto him, Father, I have sinned against heaven, and in thy sight: I am no more worthy to be called thy son. But the father said to his servants, Bring forth quickly the best robe, and put it on him; and put a ring on his hand, and shoes on his feet: and bring the fatted calf, and kill it, and let us eat, and make merry: for this my son was dead, and is alive again; he was lost, and is found. And they began to be merry. Now his elder son was in the field: and as he came and drew nigh to the house, he heard music and dancing. And he called to him one of the servants, and inquired what these things might be. And he said unto him, Thy brother is come; and thy father hath killed the fatted calf, because he hath received him safe and sound. But he was angry, and would not go in: and his father came out, and intreated him. But he answered and said to his father, Lo, these many years do I serve thee, and I never transgressed a commandment of thine: and yet thou never gavest me a kid, that I might make merry with my friends: but when this thy son came, which hath devoured thy living with harlots, thou killedst for him the fatted calf. And he said unto him, Son, thou art ever with me, and all that is mine is thine. But it was meet to make merry and be glad: for this thy brother was dead, and is alive again; and was lost, and is found.

§75 God *versus* Mammon

And Jesus said also unto the disciples, No servant can serve two masters: for either he will hate the one, and love the other; or else he will hold to one, and despise the other. Ye cannot serve God and mammon.
And the Pharisees, who were lovers of money, heard all these things; and they scoffed at Jesus. And he said unto them, Ye are they that justify yourselves in the sight of men; but God knoweth your hearts: for that which is exalted among men is an abomination in the sight of God.

§76 Parable on the Futility of Duty

And Jesus said unto his disciples, Who is there of you, having a servant plowing or keeping sheep, that will say unto him, when he is come in from the field, Come straightway and sit down to meat; and will not rather say unto him, Make ready wherewith I may sup, and gird thyself, and serve me, till I have eaten and drunken, and afterward thou shalt eat and drink? Doth he thank the servant because he did the things that were commanded? Even so ye also, when ye shall have done all the things that are commanded you, say, We are unprofitable servants; we have done that which it was our duty to do.

§77 Several Sayings of Jesus

¶The law and the prophets were until John: from that time the gospel of the kingdom of God is preached, and every man entereth violently into it. But it is easier for heaven and earth to pass away, than for one tittle of the law to fall.

¶Is it lawful on the sabbath day to do good, or to do harm? to save a life, or to kill? What man shall there be of you, that shall have one sheep, and if this fall into a pit on the sabbath day, will he not lay hold on it, and lift it out? How much then is a man of more value than a sheep! Wherefore it is lawful to do good on the sabbath day.

¶He that is not with me is against me; and he that gathereth not with me scattereth.

¶Beware of false prophets, which come to you in sheep's clothing, but inwardly are ravening wolves.

§78 Parable on Deferred Judgement

And Jesus spake this parable; A certain man had a fig tree planted in his vineyard; and he came seeking fruit thereon, and found none. And he said unto the vinedresser, Behold, these three years I come seeking fruit on this fig tree, and find none: cut it down; why doth it also cumber the ground? And he answering saith unto him, Sir, let it alone this year also, till I shall dig about it, and manure it: and if it bear fruit thenceforth, well; but if not, thou shalt cut it down.

§79 Time of the Kingdom of God

And it came to pass, as Jesus was on the way to Jerusalem, that he was passing through the midst of Samaria and Galilee.

And being asked by the Pharisees, when the kingdom of God cometh, Jesus answered them and said, The kingdom of God cometh not with observation: neither shall they say, Lo, here! or, There! for lo, the kingdom of God is in the midst of you.

And he said unto them, Verily I say unto you, There be some here of them that stand by, which shall in no wise taste of death, till they see the kingdom of God come with power.

§80 Parables on Importunity in Prayer

And Jesus spake a parable unto them to the end that they ought always to pray, and not to faint; saying, There was in a city a judge, which feared not God, and regarded not man: and there was a widow in that city; and she came oft unto him, saying, Do me justice of mine adversary. And he would not for a while: but afterward he said within himself, Though I fear not God, nor regard man; yet because this widow troubleth me, I will do her justice, lest she wear me out by her continual coming.

And Jesus said unto them, Which of you shall have a friend, and shall go unto him at midnight, and say to him, Friend, lend me three loaves; for a friend of mine is come to me from a journey, and I have nothing to set before him; and he from within shall answer and say, Trouble me not: the door is now shut, and my children are with me in bed; I cannot rise and give thee? I say unto you, Though he will not rise and give him, because he is his friend, yet because of his importunity he will arise and give him as many as he needeth.

§81 Several Sayings of Jesus

¶Have faith in God. All things are possible to him that believeth. If ye have faith as a grain of mustard seed, ye would say unto this sycamine tree, Be thou rooted up, and be thou planted in the sea; and it would have obeyed you.

¶A city set on a hill cannot be hid. Even so let your light shine before men, that they may see your good works, and glorify your Father.

¶Give, and it shall be given unto you; good measure, pressed down, shaken together, running over. For with what measure ye mete, it shall be measured unto you. Freely ye received, freely give.

¶Verily I say unto you, Inasmuch as ye did it unto one of these my brethren, even these least, ye did it unto me.

§82 Parable on the Basis of Justification

And Jesus spake also this parable unto certain which

trusted in themselves that they were righteous, and set all others at nought:
Two men went up into the temple to pray; the one a Pharisee, and the other a publican. The Pharisee stood and prayed thus with himself, God, I thank thee, that I am not as the rest of men, extortioners, unjust, adulterers, or even as this publican. I fast twice in the week; I give tithes of all that I get. But the publican, standing afar off, would not lift up so much as his eyes unto heaven, but smote his breast, saying, God, be merciful to me a sinner.
I say unto you, This man went down to his house justified rather than the other.

TEACHING AND JOURNEYING ON TO JERUSALEM † † † †

Chapter XIV: Teaching and Journeying on to Jerusalem

§83 Teachings About Divorce

AND there came Pharisees unto Jesus, and asked him, Is it lawful for a man to put away his wife? And Jesus answered and said unto them, What did Moses command you? And they said, Moses suffered to write a bill of divorcement, and to put her away. But Jesus said unto them, For your hardness of heart he wrote you this commandment.

But from the beginning of the creation, Male and female made he them. For this cause shall a man leave his father and mother, and shall cleave to his wife; and the twain shall become one flesh: so that they are no more twain, but one flesh. What therefore God hath joined together, let not man put asunder.

¶ And in the house the disciples asked Jesus again of this matter. And he saith unto them, Whosoever shall put away his wife, and marry another, committeth adultery: and if she herself shall put away her husband, and marry another, she committeth adultery.

§84 Essential for Entrance into Kingdom

And they brought unto Jesus little children: and the disciples rebuked them. But when Jesus saw it, he was moved with indignation, and said unto them, Suffer the little children to come unto me; forbid them not: for of such is the kingdom of God. Verily I say unto you, Whosoever shall not receive the kingdom of God as a little child, he shall in no wise enter therein.

§85 Relation of Possessions to Eternal Life

And as Jesus was going forth into the way, there ran one to him, and kneeled to him, and asked him, Good Teacher, what shall I do that I may inherit eternal life? And Jesus said unto him, Why callest thou me good? none is good save one, even God. Thou knowest the commandments, Do not kill, Do not commit adultery, Do not steal, Do not bear false witness, Do not defraud, Honour thy father and mother.

And he said unto him, Teacher, all these things have I observed from my youth. And Jesus looking upon him loved him, and said unto him, One thing thou lackest: go, sell whatsoever thou hast, and give to the poor, and thou shalt have treasure in heaven: and come, follow me. But his countenance fell at the saying, and he went away sorrowful: for he was one that had great possessions.

¶ And Jesus looked round about, and saith unto his disciples, How hardly shall they that have riches enter into the kingdom of God! It is easier for a camel to go through a needle's eye, than for a rich man to enter into the kingdom of God.

And the disciples were amazed at his words. But Jesus answereth again, and saith unto them, Children, how hard is it to enter into the kingdom of God!

¶ Peter began to say unto him, Lo, we have left all, and have followed thee. Jesus said, Verily I say unto you, There is no man that hath left house, or brethren, or sisters, or mother, or father, or wife, or children, or lands, but he shall receive a hundredfold now in this time, and shall inherit eternal life.

§86 Parable on the Basis of Reward

A householder went out early in the morning to hire labourers into his vineyard. And when he had agreed with the labourers for a denarius a day, he sent them into his vineyard. And he went out about the third hour, and saw others standing in the marketplace idle; and to them he said, Go ye also into the vineyard, and whatsoever is right I will give you. And they went their way. Again he went out about the sixth and the ninth hour, and did likewise. And about the eleventh hour he went out, and found others standing; and he saith unto them, Why stand ye here all the day idle? They say unto him, Because no man hath hired us. He saith unto them, Go ye also into the vineyard.

And when even was come, the owner of the vineyard saith unto his steward, Call the labourers, and pay them their hire, beginning from the last unto the first. And when they came that were hired about the eleventh hour, they received every man a denarius. And when the first came, they supposed that they would receive more; and they likewise received every man a denarius. And when they received it, they murmured against the householder, saying, These last have spent but one hour, and thou hast made them equal unto us, which have borne the burden of the day and the scorching heat. But he answered and said to one of them, Friend, I do thee no wrong: didst not thou agree with me for a denarius? Take up that which is thine, and go thy way; it is my will to give unto this last, even as unto thee.

§87 Teaching on Standards of Greatness

And they were in the way, going up to Jerusalem; and Jesus was going before them: and they were amazed; and they that followed were afraid.

¶ And there come near unto him James and John, the sons of Zebedee, saying unto him, Teacher, we would that thou shouldest do for us whatsoever we shall ask of thee. And Jesus said unto them, What would ye that I should do for you? And they said unto him, Grant unto us that we may sit, one on thy right hand, and one on thy left hand, in thy kingdom.

But Jesus said unto them, Ye know not what ye ask. Are ye able to drink the cup that I drink? or to be baptized with the baptism that I am baptized with? And they said unto him, We are able. And Jesus said unto them, The cup that I drink ye shall drink; and with the baptism that I am baptized withal shall ye be baptized: but to sit on my right hand or on my left hand is not mine to give.

¶ And when the ten heard it, they began to be moved with indignation concerning James and John. And Jesus called them to him, and saith unto them, Ye know that they which are accounted to rule over the Gentiles lord it over them; and their great ones exercise authority over them. But it is not so among you: but whosoever would become great among you, shall be your minister: and whosoever would be first among you, shall be servant of all.

For whether is greater, he that sitteth at meat, or he that serveth? is not he that sitteth at meat? but I am in the midst of you as he that serveth.

§88 The Rich Publican of Jericho

And Jesus entered and was passing through Jericho. And behold, a man called by name Zacchæus; and he was a chief publican, and he was rich. And he sought to see Jesus who he was; and could not for the crowd, because he was little of stature. And he ran on before, and climbed up into a sycomore tree to see him: for he was to pass that way.

And when Jesus came to the place, he looked up, and said unto him, Zacchæus, make haste, and come down; for to-day I must abide at thy house. And he made haste, and came down, and received Jesus joyfully.

And when they saw it, they all murmured, saying, He is gone in to lodge with a man that is a sinner.

And Zacchæus stood, and said unto the Master, Behold, Master, the half of my goods I give to the poor; and if I have wrongfully exacted aught of any man, I restore fourfold.

And Jesus said unto him, To-day is salvation come to this house, forasmuch as he also is a son of Abraham.

§89 Time of the Kingdom of God

And as they heard these things, Jesus added and spake a parable, because he was nigh to Jerusalem, and because they supposed that the kingdom of God was immediately to appear.

Jesus said therefore, A certain nobleman went into a far country. And he called ten servants of his, and gave them ten pounds, and said unto them, Trade ye herewith till I come. And it came to pass, when he was come back again, that he commanded these servants, unto whom he had given the money, to be called to him, that he might know what they had gained by trading. And the first came before him, saying, Sir, thy pound hath made ten pounds more. And he said unto him, Well done, thou good servant: because thou wast found faithful in a very little, have thou authority over ten cities. And the second came, saying, Thy pound, Sir, hath made five pounds. And he said unto him also, Be thou also over five cities. And another came, saying, Sir, behold, here is thy pound, which I kept laid up in a napkin: for I feared thee, because thou art an austere man: thou takest up that thou layedst not down, and reapest that thou didst not sow. He saith unto him, Out of thine own mouth will I judge thee. Thou knewest that I am an austere man, taking up that I laid not down, and reaping that I did not sow; then wherefore gavest thou not my money into the bank, and I, on my return, should have required it with interest? And he said unto them that stood by, Take away from him the pound, and give it unto him that hath the ten pounds.

And when Jesus had thus spoken, he went on before, going up to Jerusalem.

CHALLENGE OF THE JERUSALEM LEADERS BY JESUS † † †

Chapter XV: Challenge of the Jerusalem Leaders by Jesus

§90 Jesus Enters Jerusalem as Popular Leader

AND as Jesus was now drawing nigh unto Jerusalem, even at the descent of the mount of Olives, the whole multitude of the disciples began to rejoice and praise God with a loud voice for all the mighty works which they had seen; saying, Blessed is he that cometh in the name of the Lord: peace in heaven, and glory in the highest.

And some of the Pharisees from the multitude said unto him, Teacher, rebuke thy disciples. And he answered and said, I tell you that, if these shall hold their peace, the stones will cry out.

And when Jesus drew nigh unto Jerusalem, he saw the city and wept over it, saying,

O Jerusalem, Jerusalem, which killeth the prophets, and stoneth them that are sent unto her! how often would I have gathered thy children together, even as a hen gathereth her chickens under her wings, and ye would not! Behold, your house is left unto you desolate, till ye shall say, Blessed is he that cometh in the name of the Lord.

If thou hadst known in this day, even thou, the things which belong unto peace! but now they are hid from thine eyes. For the days shall come upon thee, when thine enemies shall cast up a bank about thee, and compass thee round, and keep thee in on every side, and shall dash thee to the ground, and thy children within thee; and they shall not leave in thee one stone upon another; because thou knewest not the time of thy visitation.

And when Jesus was come into Jerusalem, all the city was stirred, saying, Who is this? And the multitudes said, This is the prophet, Jesus, from Nazareth of Galilee.

And he entered into Jerusalem, into the temple; and when he had looked round about upon all things, it being now eventide, he went out unto Bethany with the twelve.

§91 Jesus Casts Commerce from the Temple

And on the morrow they come to Jerusalem: and Jesus entered into the temple, and began to cast out them that sold and them that bought in the temple, and overthrew the tables of the money-changers, and the seats of them that sold the doves; and he would not suffer that any man should carry a vessel through the temple.

And Jesus taught, and said unto them, Is it not written, My house shall be called a house of prayer for all the nations? but ye have made it a den of robbers.

§92 Jesus Teaches in the Temple

And Jesus was teaching daily in the temple. But the chief priests and the scribes and the principal men of the people sought to destroy him, for they feared him. And they could not find what they might do; for the people all hung upon him, listening. For all the multitude was astonished at his teaching. And every evening he went forth out of the city to Bethany, and lodged there.

§93 Jewish Rulers Challenge Authority of Jesus

And they come again to Jerusalem: and as Jesus was teaching the people in the temple, there come to him the chief priests, and the scribes, and the elders; and they said unto him, Tell us: By what authority doest thou these things? or who gave thee this authority?
And Jesus said unto them, I will ask of you one question, and answer me, and I will tell you by what authority I do these things. The baptism of John, was it from heaven, or from men? answer me.
And they reasoned with themselves, saying, If we shall say, From heaven; he will say, Why then did ye not believe him? But if we shall say, From men; all the people will stone us: for they be persuaded that John was a prophet.
And they answered Jesus and say, We know not. And Jesus saith unto them, Neither tell I you by what authority I do these things.

§94 Parables in Condemnation of Jewish Leaders

And Jesus began to speak unto them in parables:
¶ A man had two sons; and he came to the first, and said, Son, go work to-day in the vineyard. And he answered and said, I will not: but afterward he repented himself, and went. And he came to the second, and said likewise. And he answered and said, I go, sir: and went not.
What think ye? Whether of the twain did the will

of his father? They say, The first.
Jesus saith unto them, Verily I say unto you, that the publicans and the harlots go into the kingdom of God before you. For John came unto you in the way of righteousness, and ye believed him not: but the publicans and the harlots believed him: and ye, when ye saw it, did not even repent yourselves afterward, that ye might believe him.

¶Hear another parable: There was a man that was a householder, which planted a vineyard, and set a hedge about it, and digged a pit for the winepress in it, and built a tower, and let it out to husbandmen, and went into another country. And at the season of the fruits he sent to the husbandmen a servant, that he might receive from the husbandmen of the fruits of the vineyard. And they took him, and beat him, and sent him away empty. And again he sent unto them another servant; and him they wounded in the head, and handled shamefully, and sent him away empty. And he sent another; and him they killed: and many others; beating some, and killing some. And the owner of the vineyard said, What shall I do? I will send my son: it may be they will reverence him. But when the husbandmen saw him, they reasoned one with another, saying, This is the heir: let us kill him, and take his inheritance. And they cast him forth out of the vineyard, and killed him. What therefore will the owner of the vineyard do unto them? He will come and destroy these husbandmen, and will give the vineyard unto others.

¶And Jesus spake again a parable unto them, saying,

A certain king made a marriage feast for his son, and sent forth his servants to call them that were bidden to the marriage feast: and they would not come. Again he sent forth other servants, saying, Tell them that are bidden, Behold, I have made ready my dinner: my oxen and my fatlings are killed, and all things are ready: come to the marriage feast. But they made light of it, and went their ways, one to his own farm, another to his merchandise. Then saith he to his servants, The wedding is ready, but they that were bidden were not worthy. Go ye therefore unto the partings of the highways, and as many as ye shall find, bid to the marriage feast. And those servants went out into the highways, and gathered together all as many as they found: and the wedding was filled with guests.

¶ And when the chief priests and the scribes and the Pharisees heard his parables, they perceived that he spake the parables against them. And when they sought to lay hold on him in that very hour, they feared the multitudes, because they took Jesus for a prophet.

§95 Efforts to Accumulate Evidence Against Jesus

And they watched Jesus, and sent forth spies, which feigned themselves to be righteous, that they might take hold of his speech, so as to deliver him up to the rule and to the authority of the governor.

And when they were come, they say unto him, Teacher, we know that thou art true, and sayest and teachest rightly, and carest not for any one: for thou regardest not the person of men, but of a truth teachest the way of God. Tell us therefore, What thinkest thou? Is it lawful for us to give tribute unto Cæsar, or not? Shall we give, or shall we not give?

But Jesus perceived their craftiness, and said, Shew me the tribute money. And they brought unto him a denarius. And he saith unto them, Whose is this image and superscription? They say unto him, Cæsar's. Then saith he unto them, Render unto Cæsar the things that are Cæsar's; and unto God the things that are God's.

And they were not able to take hold of the saying before the people: and they marvelled at his answer, and held their peace.

¶ And there came to Jesus certain of the Sadducees, they which say that there is no resurrection; and they asked him, saying, Teacher, Moses wrote unto us, that if a man's brother die, having a wife, and he be childless, his brother should take the wife, and raise up seed unto his brother. There were seven brethren: and the first took a wife, and died childless; and the second; and the third took her; and likewise the seven also left no children, and died. Afterward the woman also died. In the resurrection whose wife of them shall she be? for the seven had her to wife.

Jesus said unto them, Is it not for this cause that ye err, that ye know not the scriptures, nor the power of God? The sons of this world marry, and are given in marriage: but they that are accounted worthy to attain to that world, and the resurrection from the dead, neither marry, nor are given in marriage: for neither can they die any more: for they are equal unto the angels; and are sons of God, being sons of the resurrection.

But that the dead are raised, even Moses shewed when he calleth the Lord the God of Abraham, and the God of Isaac, and the God of Jacob. Now he is not the God of the dead, but of the living: for all live unto him. Ye do greatly err.

And when the multitudes heard it, they were astonished at his teaching.

¶ And the scribes and the Pharisees bring a woman taken in adultery; and having set her in the midst, they say unto him, Teacher, this woman hath been taken in adultery, in the very act. Now in the law Moses commanded us to stone such: what then sayest thou of her?

And this they said, trying him, that they might have whereof to accuse him.

But Jesus stooped down, and with his finger wrote on the ground. But when they continued asking him, he lifted up himself, and said unto them, He that is without sin among you, let him first cast a stone at her. And again he stooped down, and with his finger wrote on the ground. And they, when they heard it, went out one by one, beginning from the eldest, even unto the last: and Jesus was left alone, and the woman, where she was, in the midst. And Jesus lifted up himself, and said unto her, Woman, where are they? did no man condemn thee? And she said, No man, Master. And Jesus said, Neither do I condemn thee: go thy way; from henceforth sin no more.

¶ And one of the scribes came, and heard them ques-

tioning together, and knowing that Jesus had answered them well, asked him a question: Teacher, What commandment is the first of all?
Jesus answered, The first is, Hear, O Israel; The Lord our God, the Lord is one: and thou shalt love the Lord thy God with all thy heart, and with all thy soul, and with all thy mind, and with all thy strength. The second is this, Thou shalt love thy neighbour as thyself. There is none other commandment greater than these.
And the scribe said unto Jesus, Of a truth, Teacher, thou hast well said that he is one; and there is none other but he: and to love him with all the heart, and with all the understanding, and with all the strength, and to love his neighbour as himself, is much more than all whole burnt offerings and sacrifices.
And when Jesus saw that he answered discreetly, he said unto him, Thou art not far from the kingdom of God.
And no man after that durst ask Jesus any question.

DISCOURSE IN CONDEMNATION OF SCRIBES AND PHARISEES † †

Chapter XVI: Discourse in Condemnation of Scribes and Pharisees

§96 Discourse in Condemnation of Scribes and Pharisees

THEN spake Jesus to the multitudes and to his disciples, saying, Beware of the scribes, which desire to walk in long robes: they make broad their phylacteries, and enlarge the borders of their garments. They love the chief place at feasts, and the chief seats in the synagogues, and the salutations in the marketplaces. They devour widows' houses, even while for a pretence they make long prayers. All their works they do for to be seen of men.

They love to be called of men, Rabbi. But be not ye called Rabbi: for one is your teacher, and all ye are brethren. Neither be ye called Master: for one is your master. And call no man your father on the earth: for one is your Father.

Whosoever shall exalt himself shall be humbled; and whosoever shall humble himself shall be exalted. He that is greatest among you shall be your minister.

¶Woe unto you, scribes and Pharisees, hypocrites! for ye lade men with burdens grievous to be borne, and ye yourselves touch not the burdens with one of your fingers.

Woe unto you, scribes and Pharisees, hypocrites! because ye shut the kingdom of God against men: for ye enter not in yourselves, neither suffer ye them that are entering in to enter.

Woe unto you, scribes and Pharisees, hypocrites! for ye compass sea and land to make one proselyte; and

when he is become so, ye make him twofold more a son of hell than yourselves.
Woe unto you, ye blind guides, which say, Whosoever shall swear by the temple, it is nothing; but whosoever shall swear by the gold of the temple, he is bound by his oath. Ye fools and blind: for whether is greater, the gold, or the temple that hath sanctified the gold? And, Whosoever shall swear by the altar, it is nothing; but whosoever shall swear by the gift that is upon it, he is bound by his oath. Ye blind: for whether is greater, the gift, or the altar that sanctifieth the gift?
Woe unto you, scribes and Pharisees, hypocrites! for ye tithe mint and anise and cummin, and have left undone the weightier matters of the law, justice, and mercy, and integrity. Ye blind guides, which strain out the gnat, and swallow the camel.
Woe unto you, scribes and Pharisees, hypocrites! for ye cleanse the outside of the cup and of the platter, but within they are full from extortion and excess. Thou blind Pharisee, cleanse first the inside of the cup and of the platter, that the outside thereof may become clean also.
Woe unto you, scribes and Pharisees, hypocrites! for ye are like unto whited sepulchres, which outwardly appear beautiful, but inwardly are full of dead men's bones, and of all uncleanness. Ye outwardly appear righteous unto men, but inwardly ye are full of hypocrisy and iniquity.
Woe unto you, scribes and Pharisees, hypocrites! for ye build the sepulchres of the prophets, and garnish the tombs of the righteous, and say, If we had been

in the days of our fathers, we should not have been partakers with them in the blood of the prophets. Wherefore ye witness to yourselves, that ye are sons of them that slew the prophets. Fill ye up then the measure of your fathers.

¶And the scribes and the Pharisees began to press upon Jesus vehemently, and to provoke him to speak of many things; laying wait for him, to catch something out of his mouth.

§97 The True Test of Giving

And Jesus sat down over against the treasury, and beheld how the multitude cast money into the treasury: and many that were rich cast in much. And there came a poor widow, and she cast in small copper coins. And Jesus called unto him his disciples, and said unto them, Verily I say unto you, This poor widow cast in more than all they which are casting into the treasury: for they all did cast in of their superfluity; but she of her want did cast in all that she had.

DISCOURSE ON EVENTS OF THE FUTURE † † † † †

Chapter XVII: Discourse on Events of the Future

§98 Discourse on Events of the Future

AND as Jesus went forth out of the temple, one of his disciples saith unto him, Teacher, behold, what manner of stones and what manner of buildings!

And Jesus said unto him, Seest thou these great buildings? there shall not be left here one stone upon another, which shall not be thrown down.

¶ And as Jesus sat on the mount of Olives over against the temple, Peter and James and John and Andrew asked him privately, Tell us, when shall these things be? and what shall be the sign when these things are about to be accomplished?

¶ And Jesus began to say unto them, When ye shall hear of wars and rumours of wars, be not troubled: these things must needs come to pass. For nation shall rise against nation, and kingdom against kingdom: there shall be famines and pestilences. These things are the beginning of travail: but the end is not yet.

¶ But when ye see the abomination of desolation standing where he ought not (let him that readeth understand), then let them that are in Judæa flee unto the mountains. And let them that are in the midst of Jerusalem depart out. And let not them that are in the country enter therein. For these are days of vengeance. Woe unto them that are with child and to them that give suck in those days! And pray ye that your flight be not in the winter. For those days shall be tribulation, such as there hath not been the like from the beginning of the creation which God created until now, and never shall be.

¶Now from the fig tree learn her parable: when her branch is now become tender, and putteth forth its leaves, ye know that the summer is nigh. Verily I say unto you, This generation shall not pass away, until all these things be accomplished.

¶The days will come, when ye shall desire to see the Day of the Son of man, and ye shall not see it. And they shall say to you, Lo, there! Lo, here! go not away nor follow after them.

Take heed that no man lead you astray. For many shall come, saying, I am the Christ; and, The time is at hand. They shall lead many astray. Go ye not after them.

¶For as the lightning, when it
 lighteneth out of the one part under the heaven,
 shineth unto the other part under heaven;
so shall the Son of man be in his Day.
As it came to pass in the days of Noah,
even so shall it be also in the Day of the Son of man.
 They ate, they drank, they married, they were given in marriage, until the day that Noah entered into the ark, and the flood came, and destroyed them all.
Likewise even as it came to pass in the days of Lot;
 They ate, they drank, they bought, they sold, they planted, they builded; but in the day that Lot went out from Sodom it rained fire and brimstone from heaven, and destroyed them all.
After the same manner shall it be in the Day that the Son of man is revealed.

In that day,
he which shall be on the housetop,
and his goods in the house, let him not go down
to take them away: and let
him that is in the field
likewise not return back.
In that night
there shall be two men on one bed;
the one shall be taken, and the other shall be left;
there shall be two women grinding together;
the one shall be taken, and the other shall be left.
¶ And they answering say unto Jesus,
Where, Master?
And Jesus said unto them,
Where the carcase is, thither will the vultures also
be gathered together.
¶ But of that Day knoweth no one, not even the angels
in heaven, neither the Son, but the Father.
Take ye heed: for ye know not when the time is.
It is as when ten virgins took their lamps, and went forth to meet the bridegroom. And five of them were foolish, and five were wise. For the foolish, when they took their lamps, took no oil with them: but the wise took oil in their vessels with their lamps. Now while the bridegroom tarried, they all slumbered and slept. But at midnight there is a cry, Behold, the bridegroom! Come ye forth to meet him. Then all those virgins arose, and trimmed their lamps. And the foolish said unto the wise, Give us of your oil; for our lamps are going out. But the wise answered, saying, Peradventure there will not be enough for us and you: go ye

rather to them that sell, and buy for yourselves. And while they went away to buy, the bridegroom came.
¶ Take ye heed to yourselves: for they shall deliver you up to councils; and in synagogues shall ye be beaten; and before governors and kings shall ye stand. It shall turn unto you for a testimony.

And when they lead you to judgement, and deliver you up, be not anxious beforehand what ye shall speak: but whatsoever shall be given you in that hour, that speak ye. For it is not ye that speak, but the Spirit of your Father that speaketh in you.

And brother shall deliver up brother to death, and the father his child; and children shall rise up against parents, and cause them to be put to death. And ye shall be hated of all men. In your patience ye shall win your lives.

Behold, I send you forth as sheep in the midst of wolves: be ye therefore wise as serpents, and harmless as doves.

A disciple is not above his teacher. It is enough for the disciple that he be as his teacher. If they have called the master of the house Beelzebub, how much more shall they call them of his household!

There is nothing covered up, that shall not be revealed: and hid, that shall not be known. What I tell you in the darkness, speak ye in the light: and what ye hear in the ear, proclaim upon the housetops.

And I say unto you my friends, Be not afraid of them which kill the body, and after that have no more that they can do. Are not five sparrows sold for two farthings? and not one of them is forgotten in the sight of

God. But the very hairs of your head are all numbered. Fear not: ye are of more value than many sparrows. Every one who shall confess me before men, him will I also confess before my Father. But whosoever shall deny me before men, him will I also deny before my Father. He that heareth you heareth me; and he that rejecteth you rejecteth me; and he that rejecteth me rejecteth him that sent me.

¶ For it is as when a man, going into another country, called his own servants, and delivered unto them his goods. And unto one he gave five talents, and to another two, to another one; to each according to his several ability; and he went on his journey.

Straightway he that received the five talents went and traded with them, and made other five talents. In like manner he also that received the two gained other two. But he that received the one went away and digged in the earth, and hid his master's money.

Now after a long time the master of those servants cometh, and maketh a reckoning with them.

And he that received the five talents came and brought other five talents, saying, Sir, thou deliveredst unto me five talents: lo, I have gained other five talents. His master said unto him, Well done, good and faithful servant: thou hast been faithful over a few things, I will set thee over many things.

And he also that received the two talents came and said, Sir, thou deliveredst unto me two talents: lo, I have gained other two talents. His master said unto him, Well done, good and faithful servant; thou hast

been faithful over a few things, I will set thee over many things.
And he also that had received the one talent came and said, Sir, I knew thee that thou art a hard man, reaping where thou didst not sow, and gathering where thou didst not scatter: and I was afraid, and went away and hid thy talent in the earth: lo, thou hast thine own. But his master answered and said unto him, Thou wicked and slothful servant, thou knewest that I reap where I sowed not, and gather where I did not scatter; thou oughtest therefore to have put my money to the bankers, and at my coming I should have received back mine own with interest.
Take ye away therefore the talent from him, and give it unto him that hath the ten talents.
To whomsoever much is given, of him shall much be required.

§99 Teaching by Jesus in Jerusalem

And every day Jesus was teaching in the temple; and every night he went out, and lodged in the mount that is called the mount of Olives. And all the people came early in the morning to him in the temple, to hear him.

FINAL HOURS OF JESUS WITH HIS DISCIPLES † † †

Chapter XVIII: Final Hours of Jesus With His Disciples

§100 Conspiracy for the Arrest of Jesus

NOW after two days was the feast of the passover and the unleavened bread. And the chief priests and the scribes sought how they might take Jesus with subtilty, and kill him. But they said, Not during the feast, lest haply there shall be a tumult of the people. And Judas Iscariot, he that was one of the twelve, went away unto the chief priests, that he might deliver Jesus unto them. And they, when they heard it, were glad, and promised to give him money. And he sought how he might conveniently deliver Jesus unto them in the absence of the multitude.

§101 The Passover with the Disciples

And the day of unleavened bread came, on which the passover must be sacrificed. And Jesus sent Peter and John, saying, Go and make ready for us the passover, that we may eat. And they said unto him, Where wilt thou that we make ready? And Jesus said, Go into the city to such a man, and say unto him, The Teacher saith, My time is at hand; I keep the passover at thy house with my disciples. And the disciples did as Jesus appointed them; and they made ready the passover.
And when the hour was come, Jesus sat down, and the twelve with him. And he said unto them,
With desire I have desired to eat this passover with you before I suffer: for I say unto you, I will not eat it, until it be fulfilled in the kingdom of God.
And he received a cup, and when he had given thanks,

he said, Take this, and divide it among yourselves: for I say unto you, I will not drink from henceforth of the fruit of the vine, until that day when I drink it new in the kingdom of God.
Behold, the hand of him that betrayeth me is with me on the table. And they began to question among themselves, which of them it was that should do this thing.

§ 102 Withdrawal to the Mount of Olives

And when they had sung a hymn, they went out unto the mount of Olives. And Jesus saith unto them, All ye shall be offended: for it is written, I will smite the shepherd, and the sheep shall be scattered abroad. But Peter said unto him, Although all shall be offended, yet will not I. And Jesus saith unto him, Verily I say unto thee, that thou to-day, even this night, before the cock crow, shalt deny me. But he spake exceeding vehemently, If I must die with thee, I will not deny thee. And in like manner also said they all.

§ 103 At the Place Named Gethsemane

And they come unto a place which was named Gethsemane: and Jesus saith unto his disciples, Sit ye here, while I pray. And he taketh with him Peter and James and John, and began to be greatly agitated, and sore troubled. And he saith unto them, My soul is exceeding sorrowful even unto death: abide ye here, and watch.
And Jesus went forward a little, and fell on the ground, and prayed that, if it were possible, the hour might

pass away from him. And he said, Abba, Father, all things are possible unto thee; remove this cup from me: howbeit not what I will, but what thou wilt.
And he cometh, and findeth them sleeping, and saith unto Peter, Simon, sleepest thou? couldest thou not watch one hour? Watch and pray, that ye enter not into temptation: the spirit indeed is willing, but the flesh is weak.
And again Jesus went away, and prayed, saying, O my Father, if this cannot pass away, except I drink it, thy will be done. And again he came, and found them sleeping, for their eyes were very heavy; and they wist not what to answer him.
And Jesus left them again, and went away, and prayed a third time, saying again the same words. Then cometh he to the disciples, and saith unto them, Sleep on now, and take your rest: it is enough: the hour is at hand. Arise, let us be going: behold, he is at hand that betrayeth me.

§104 Betrayal and Arrest of Jesus

And straightway, while Jesus yet spake, cometh Judas, one of the twelve, and with him a multitude with swords and staves, from the chief priests and the scribes and the elders.
Now he that betrayed Jesus had given them a token, saying, Whomsoever I shall kiss, that is he; take him, and lead him away safely. And when he was come, straightway Judas came to him, and saith, Rabbi; and kissed him. And they laid hands on Jesus, and took him.

And behold, one of them that were with Jesus stretched out his hand, and drew his sword, and smote the servant of the high priest. Then saith Jesus unto him, Put up again thy sword into its place: for all they that take the sword shall perish with the sword.
And Jesus said unto the chief priests, and captains of the temple, and elders, which were come against him, Are ye come out, as against a robber, with swords and staves? When I was daily with you in the temple, ye stretched not forth your hands against me: but this is your hour, and the power of darkness.
Then all the disciples left Jesus, and fled.

JUDICIAL TRIALS AND CRUCIFIXION OF JESUS † † † †

Chapter XIX: Judicial Trials and Crucifixion of Jesus

§105 The Trial Before the Jewish Authorities

AND they seized Jesus, and led him away, and brought him into the high priest's house. But Peter followed afar off. And when they had kindled a fire in the midst of the court, and had sat down together, Peter sat in the midst of them. And a certain maid seeing him as he sat in the light of the fire, and looking stedfastly upon him, said, This man also was with Jesus. But he denied, saying, Woman, I know him not. And after a little while another saw him, and said, Thou also art one of them. But Peter said, Man, I am not. And after the space of about one hour another confidently affirmed, saying, Of a truth this man also was with Jesus: for he is a Galilæan. But Peter said, Man, I know not what thou sayest.

And the Master turned, and looked upon Peter. And Peter remembered the word of the Master, how that he said unto him, Before the cock crow this day, thou shalt deny me. And he went out, and wept bitterly.

And the men that held Jesus mocked him, and beat him. And they blindfolded him, and asked him, saying, Prophesy: who is he that struck thee? And many other things spake they against him, reviling him.

And as soon as it was day, the assembly of the elders of the people was gathered together, both chief priests and scribes; and they led Jesus away into their council.

Now the chief priests and the whole council sought witness against Jesus to put him to death; and found it not. For many bare false witness against him, and their witness agreed not together. And there stood up certain, and bare false witness against him, saying, We heard him say, I will destroy this temple that is made with hands, and in three days I will build another made without hands. And not even so did their witness agree together.

And the high priest stood up in the midst, and asked Jesus, saying, Answerest thou nothing? what is it which these witness against thee? But Jesus held his peace, and answered nothing.

Again the high priest asked Jesus, and saith unto him, If thou art the Christ, tell us. But he said unto them, If I tell you, ye will not believe: and if I ask you, ye will not answer. And they all said, Art thou the Son of God? And Jesus said unto them, Ye say that I am.

And they said, What further need have we of witness? for we ourselves have heard from his own mouth. And they all condemned him to be worthy of death.

§106 The Trial Before the Roman Authorities

And the whole company of them rose up, and brought Jesus before Pilate the governor. And they began to accuse him, saying, We found this man perverting our nation, and forbidding to give tribute to Cæsar, and saying that he himself is Christ a king. And Pilate asked him, saying, Art thou the King of the Jews? And Jesus answered him and said, Thou sayest.

And the chief priests accused him of many things. And Pilate again asked him, saying, Answerest thou nothing? behold how many things they accuse thee of. But Jesus no more answered anything; insomuch that Pilate marvelled.

And Pilate said unto the chief priests, I find no fault in this man. But they were the more urgent, saying, He stirreth up the people, teaching throughout all Judæa, and beginning from Galilee even unto this place. But when Pilate heard it, he asked whether the man were a Galilæan. And when he knew that he was of Herod's jurisdiction, he sent him unto Herod, who himself also was at Jerusalem in these days.
Now when Herod saw Jesus, he was exceeding glad: for he was of a long time desirous to see him, because he had heard concerning him. And he questioned him in many words; but Jesus answered him nothing. And the chief priests and the scribes stood, vehemently accusing him. And Herod with his soldiers set him at nought, and mocked him, and arraying him in gorgeous apparel sent him back to Pilate.
And Pilate called together the chief priests and the rulers, and said unto them, Ye brought unto me this man, as one that perverteth the people: and behold, I, having examined him before you, found no fault in this man touching those things whereof ye accuse him: no, nor yet Herod: for he sent him back unto us; and behold, nothing worthy of death hath been done by him. I will therefore chastise him and release him.
Now at the feast Pilate the governor used to release unto them one prisoner, whom they asked of him. And the multitude went up and began to ask him to do as he was wont to do unto them. And Pilate answered them, saying, Will ye that I release unto you the King of the Jews? For he perceived that for envy

the chief priests had delivered him up.

And there was one called Barabbas, a notable prisoner, lying bound in prison with them that had made insurrection, men who in the insurrection had committed murder.

And the chief priests stirred up the multitude, that he should rather release Barabbas unto them. And they cried out all together, saying, Away with this man, and release unto us Barabbas. And Pilate again answered and said unto them, What then shall I do unto him whom ye call the King of the Jews? And they cried out, Crucify him. And Pilate said unto them, Why, what evil hath he done? I have found no cause of death in him: I will therefore chastise him and release him. But they cried out exceedingly, Crucify, crucify him.

And their voices prevailed. And Pilate gave sentence that what they asked for should be done. And he released him that for insurrection and murder had been cast into prison, whom they asked for; but Jesus he delivered up to their will.

And the soldiers led Jesus away within the court, which is the Prætorium; and they call together the whole band. And they clothe him with purple, and plaiting a crown of thorns, they put it on him; and they began to salute him, Hail, King of the Jews! And they smote his head with a reed, and did spit upon him. And when they had mocked him, they took off from him the purple, and put on him his garments. And they lead him out to crucify him.

§107 The Crucifixion of Jesus

And when they led Jesus away, they laid hold upon one Simon of Cyrene, coming from the country, and laid on him the cross, to bear it after Jesus.
And there followed Jesus a great multitude of the people, and of women who bewailed and lamented him. But Jesus turning unto them said, Daughters of Jerusalem, weep not for me, but weep for yourselves, and for your children. For behold, the days are coming, in which they shall say, Blessed are the barren, and the wombs that never bare, and the breasts that never gave suck. Then shall they begin to say to the mountains, Fall on us; and to the hills, Cover us. For if they do these things in the green tree, what shall be done in the dry?
And they bring Jesus unto the place Golgotha, which is, being interpreted, The place of a skull. And they offered him wine mingled with myrrh: but he received it not. And they part his garments among them, casting lots upon them, what each should take. And it was the third hour, and they crucified him. And with him they crucify two robbers; one on his right hand, and one on his left. And the superscription of his accusation was written and set up over his head: THE KING OF THE JEWS. And they sat and watched him there.
And Jesus said, Father, forgive them; for they know not what they do.
And they that passed by railed on him, wagging their heads, and saying, Ha! thou that destroyest the temple, and buildest it in three days, save thyself, and come

down from the cross. In like manner also the chief priests mocking him among themselves with the scribes said, He saved others; himself he cannot save. Let the Christ, the King of Israel, now come down from the cross, that we may see and believe. He trusteth on God; let him deliver him now, if he desireth him.

And it was now about the ninth hour. And when Jesus had cried with a loud voice, he said, Father, into thy hands I commend my spirit: and having said this, he yielded up his spirit.

And when the centurion, which stood by over against Jesus, saw what was done, he said, Certainly this was a righteous man.

MESSIANIC INTERLUDES

MESSIANIC INTERLUDES

POLITICAL MESSIANISM

APOCALYPTIC MESSIANISM

¶ He shall be great, and shall be called the Son of the Most High: and the Lord God shall give unto him the throne of his father David: and he shall reign over the house of Jacob for ever; and of his kingdom there shall be no end.

¶ Looking for the consolation of Israel.
Looking for the redemption of Jerusalem.

¶ Where is he that is born King of the Jews?
Where should the Christ be born?

¶ And thou Bethlehem, land of Judah,
Art in no wise least among the princes of Judah:
For out of thee shall come forth a governor,
Which shall be shepherd of my people Israel.

¶ Blessed be the Lord, the God of Israel;
For he hath visited and wrought redemption for his people,
And hath raised up a horn of salvation for us,
Salvation from our enemies, and from the hand of all that hate us;
To grant unto us that we being delivered out of the hand of our enemies
Should serve him without fear,

In holiness and righteousness before him all our
days.

¶ Hosanna to the son of David! Blessed is the King that cometh in the name of the Lord, even the King of Israel. Blessed is the kingdom that cometh, the kingdom of our father David. Hosanna in the highest!

¶ Art thou the Christ, the Son of the Blessed?
He says that he himself is Christ a king.
Art thou the King of the Jews?
Will ye that I release unto you the King of the Jews?
What then shall I do unto him whom ye call the King of the Jews?
Hail, King of the Jews!
Ha! If thou art the King of the Jews, save thyself!
THIS IS JESUS THE KING OF THE JEWS

¶ REPENT ye; for the kingdom of heaven is at hand!
The time is fulfilled, and the kingdom of God is at hand: repent ye, and believe in the gospel!
Say unto them, The kingdom of God is come nigh unto you!
Say unto them, Howbeit know this, that the kingdom of God is come nigh!

¶ I was not sent but unto the lost sheep of the house of Israel.
Go not into any way of the Gentiles, and enter not into any city of the Samaritans: but go rather to the lost sheep of the house of Israel. And as ye go, preach, saying, The kingdom of heaven is at hand! When they persecute you in this city, flee into the next: for verily I say unto you, Ye shall not have gone through the cities of Israel, till the Son of man be come.

¶ For the Son of man shall come in the glory of his Father with his angels; and then shall he render unto every man according to his deeds. Verily I say unto you, There be some of them that stand here, which shall in no wise taste of death, till they see the Son of man coming in his kingdom.

¶ Shall not God avenge his elect, which cry to him day and night, and he is longsuffering over them? I say unto you, that he will avenge them speedily. Howbeit when the Son of man cometh, shall he find the faith on the earth?

¶ In the regeneration when the Son of man shall sit on the throne of his glory, ye also shall sit upon twelve thrones, judging the twelve tribes of Israel.

¶ There shall be terrors and great signs from heaven. There shall be signs in sun and moon and stars. The sun shall be darkened, and the moon shall not give her light, and the stars shall be falling from heaven, and the powers that are in the heavens shall be shaken. And then shall appear the sign of the Son of man in heaven. And they shall see the Son of man coming in clouds with great power and glory. And then shall he send forth the angels, and shall gather together his elect from the four winds, from the uttermost part of the earth to the uttermost part of heaven. Watch ye at every season, making supplication, that ye may prevail to escape all these things that shall come to pass, and to stand before the Son of man.

¶ Ye shall see the Son of man sitting at the right hand of the Power, and coming on the clouds of heaven.

¶ So shall it be in the end of the world: the angels shall come forth, and sever the wicked from among the righteous, and shall cast them into the furnace of fire: there shall be the weeping and gnashing of teeth.

So shall it be in the end of the world: the Son of man shall send forth his angels, and they shall gather out of his kingdom all things that cause stumbling, and them that do iniquity, and shall cast them into the furnace of fire: there shall be the weeping and gnashing of teeth. Then shall the righteous shine forth as the sun in the kingdom of their Father.

¶ When the Son of man shall come in his glory, and all the angels with him, then shall he sit on the throne of his glory: and before him shall be gathered all the nations: and he shall separate them one from another, as the shepherd separateth the sheep from the goats: and he shall set the sheep on his right hand, but the goats on the left. Then shall the King say unto them on his right hand, Come, ye blessed of my Father, inherit the kingdom prepared for you from the foundation of the world. Then shall he say also unto them on the left hand, Depart from me, ye cursed, into the eternal fire which is prepared for the devil and his angels. And these shall go away into eternal punishment: but the righteous into eternal life.

BOOK II

THE RECORD OF JOHN

Philosophy and Psychology of Religion

BOOK II: THE RECORD OF JOHN

Philosophy and Psychology of Religion

§1 Prologue to the Record of John

IN the beginning was the Word, and the Word was with God, and the Word was God. The same was in the beginning with God. All things were made through him; and without him was not anything made that hath been made. In him was life; and the life was the light of men. And the light shineth in the darkness; and the darkness apprehended it not.
There was the true light. He was in the world, and the world was made through him, and the world knew him not. He came unto his own, and they that were his own received him not. But as many as received him, to them gave he the right to become children of God, which were begotten, not of blood, nor of the will of the flesh, nor of the will of man, but of God.
The Word became flesh, and dwelt among us, full of grace and truth. Of his fulness we all received, and grace for grace. For the law was given by Moses; grace and truth came through Jesus Christ.

§2 With a Jewish Teacher

Now there was a man of the Pharisees, named Nicodemus, a ruler of the Jews: the same came unto Jesus by night, and said to him, Rabbi, we know that thou art a teacher come from God: for no man can do what thou doest, except God be with him. Jesus answered and said unto him, Verily, verily, I say unto thee, Except a man be born anew, he cannot see the kingdom of God. Nicodemus saith unto him, How can a man be born when he is old? can he enter a second time into his mother's womb, and be born? Jesus answered, Verily, verily, I say unto thee, Except a man be born of the Spirit, he cannot enter into the kingdom of God. That which is born of the flesh is flesh; and that which is born of the Spirit is spirit. Marvel not that I said unto thee, Ye must be born anew. The wind bloweth where it listeth, and thou hearest the voice thereof, but knowest not whence it cometh, and whither it goeth: so is every one that is born of the Spirit. Nicodemus answered and said unto him, How can these things be? Jesus answered and said unto him, Art thou the teacher of Israel, and understandest not these things?

§3 With a Samaritan Woman

And Jesus must needs pass through Samaria. So he cometh to a city of Samaria, called Sychar, near to the parcel of ground that Jacob gave to his son Joseph: and Jacob's well was there. Jesus therefore, being wearied with his journey, sat as he was by the well. It was about the sixth hour.

There cometh a woman of Samaria to draw water: Jesus saith unto her, Give me to drink. For his disciples were gone away into the city to buy food. The Samaritan woman therefore saith unto him, How is it that thou, being a Jew, askest drink of me, which am a Samaritan woman? (For Jews have no dealings with Samaritans.)

Jesus answered and said unto her, If thou knewest the gift of God, and who it is that saith to thee, Give me to drink; thou wouldest have asked of him, and he would have given thee living water. The woman saith unto him, Sir, thou hast nothing to draw with, and the well is deep: from whence then hast thou that living water?

Jesus answered and said unto her, Every one that drinketh of this water shall thirst again: but whosoever drinketh of the water that I shall give him shall never thirst; but the water that I shall give him shall become in him a well of water springing up unto eternal life.

The woman saith unto him, Sir, give me this water, that I thirst not, neither come all the way hither to draw.

Jesus saith unto her, Go, call thy husband, and come hither.

The woman saith unto Jesus, Sir, I perceive that thou art a prophet. Our fathers worshipped in this mountain; and ye say, that in Jerusalem is the place where men ought to worship. Jesus saith unto her, Woman, believe me, the hour cometh, when neither in this mountain, nor in Jerusalem, shall ye worship the Father. But the hour cometh, and now is, when the true worshippers shall worship the Father in spirit and truth. God is a Spirit: and they that worship him must worship in spirit and truth.

§4 With the Disciples

And upon this came his disciples; and they marvelled that Jesus was speaking with a woman; yet no man said, What seekest thou? or, Why speakest thou with her?

And the disciples prayed him, saying, Rabbi, eat. But

he said unto them, I have meat to eat that ye know not. The disciples therefore said one to another, Hath any man brought him aught to eat? Jesus saith unto them, My meat is to do the will of him that sent me, and to accomplish his work.

§5 On the Bread of Life

These things said Jesus in the synagogue, as he taught in Capernaum: Work not for the meat which perisheth, but for the meat which abideth unto eternal life. They said therefore unto him, What must we do, that we may work the works of God? Jesus answered and said unto them, This is the work of God, that ye believe on him whom he hath sent. For the bread of God giveth life unto the world. They said therefore unto him, Sir, evermore give us this bread. Jesus said unto them, I am the bread of life: he that cometh to me shall not hunger. For I am come down from heaven, not to do mine own will, but the will of him that sent me.

The Jews therefore murmured concerning him, because he said, I am the bread which came down out of heaven. And they said, Is not this Jesus, the son of Joseph, whose father and mother we know? how doth he now say, I am come down out of heaven? Jesus answered and said unto them, Verily, verily, I say unto you, I am the bread of life. This is the bread which cometh down out of heaven, that a man may eat thereof, and not die. I am the living bread: if any man eat of this bread, he shall live forever.

The Jews therefore strove one with another, saying,

How can this man give us his flesh to eat? Jesus therefore said unto them, Verily, verily, I say unto you, Except ye eat my flesh and drink my blood, ye have not life in yourselves. He that eateth my flesh and drinketh my blood hath eternal life. He abideth in me, and I in him. As the living Father sent me, and I live because of the Father; so he also shall live because of me. He that eateth this bread shall live forever.
Many therefore of his disciples, when they heard this, said, This is a hard saying; who can hear it? But Jesus knowing in himself that his disciples murmured at this, said unto them, Doth this cause you to stumble? It is the spirit that quickeneth; the flesh profiteth nothing: the words that I have spoken unto you are spirit, and are life.

§6 On the Light of Life

These words spake Jesus in the treasury, as he taught in the temple, saying, I am the light of the world: he that followeth me shall not walk in the darkness, but shall have the light of life. The Pharisees therefore said unto him, Thou bearest witness of thyself. Jesus answered and said unto them, Even if I bear witness of myself, my witness is true. In your law it is written, that the witness of two men is true. I am he that beareth witness of myself, and the Father that sent me beareth witness of me.
And Jesus said, For judgement came I into this world, that they which see not may see; and that they which see may become blind. Those of the Pharisees which were with him heard these things, and said unto him,

Are we also blind? Jesus said unto them, If ye were blind, ye would have no sin: but now ye say, We see: your sin remaineth.
And this is the judgement, that the light is come into the world, and men loved the darkness rather than the light; for their works were evil. For every one that doeth ill hateth the light, and cometh not to the light, lest his works should be reproved. But he that doeth the truth cometh to the light, that his works may be made manifest, that they have been wrought in God.
Yet a little while is the light among you. Walk while ye have the light, that darkness overtake you not: and he that walketh in the darkness knoweth not whither he goeth. While ye have the light, believe on the light, that ye may become sons of light.

§7 Several Sayings of Jesus

¶Verily, verily, I say unto you, He that heareth my word, and believeth him that sent me, hath eternal life, and cometh not into judgement, but hath passed out of death into life.
¶No man can come to me, except the Father draw him. Every one that hath heard from the Father, and hath learned, cometh unto me.
¶My judgement is righteous; because I seek not mine own will, but the will of him that sent me.
¶Ye search the scriptures, because ye think that in them ye have eternal life; and ye will not come to me, that ye may have life.
¶He that sent me is with me; he hath not left me

alone; for I do always the things that are pleasing to him.

¶ Verily, verily, I say unto you, Before Abraham was, I am.

§8 On Freedom through Truth

Jesus said to those Jews which had believed him, If ye abide in my word, then are ye truly my disciples; and ye shall know the truth, and the truth shall make you free. They answered unto him, We be Abraham's seed, and have never yet been in bondage to any man: how sayest thou, Ye shall be made free? Jesus answered them, Verily, verily, I say unto you, Every one that committeth sin is the bondservant of sin.

§9 On Life through Loyalty

Jesus said, Verily, verily, I say unto you, If a man keep my word, he shall never see death. The Jews said unto him, Abraham is dead, and the prophets; and thou sayest, If a man keep my word, he shall never taste of death. Art thou greater than our father Abraham, which is dead? and the prophets are dead: whom makest thou thyself? Jesus answered, If I glorify myself, my glory is nothing: it is my Father that glorifieth me. I know him, and keep his word.

§10 On Jesus as Son

For this cause did the Jews persecute Jesus, because he did things on the sabbath. But Jesus answered them, My Father worketh even until now, and I work. For this cause therefore the Jews sought the more to kill him, because he not only brake the sabbath, but also called God his own Father, making himself equal with God.

Jesus therefore answered and said unto them, I and the Father are one. The Jews took up stones to stone him. Jesus answered them, Many good works have I shewed you from the Father; for which of those works do ye stone me? The Jews answered him, For a good work we stone thee not, but for blasphemy; and because that thou, being a man, makest thyself God.

Jesus answered them, If I do not the works of my Father, believe me not. But if I do them, though ye believe not me, believe the works: that ye may know and understand that the Father is in me, and I in the Father.

§11 Several Sayings of Jesus

¶I am the resurrection, and the life: he that believeth on me, though he die, yet shall he live: and whosoever liveth and believeth on me shall never die.

¶I came that they may have life, and may have it abundantly.

¶This is life eternal: that they should know the only true God.

¶Verily, verily, I say unto you, Except a grain of wheat fall into the earth and die, it abideth by itself alone; but if it die, it beareth much fruit. He that loveth his life loseth it; and he that hateth his life shall keep it.

§12 Source of the Teaching

And Jesus cried and said, He that believeth on me, believeth not on me, but on him that sent me. And

he that beholdeth me beholdeth him that sent me.
And if any man hear my sayings, and keep them not, I judge him not: for I came not to judge the world. He that rejecteth me, and receiveth not my sayings, hath one that judgeth him: the word that I spake, the same shall judge him.
For I spake not from myself; but the Father which sent me, he hath given me a commandment, what I should say, and what I should speak. And I know that his commandment is life eternal: the things therefore which I speak, even as the Father hath said unto me, so I speak.

§13 Test for the Teaching

When it was now the midst of the feast Jesus went up into the temple, and taught. The Jews therefore marvelled, saying, How knoweth this man letters, having never learned? Jesus therefore answered them, and said, My teaching is not mine, but his that sent me. If any man willeth to do his will, he shall know of the teaching, whether it be of God, or whether I speak from myself.

§14 Estimate of the Teaching

The officers came to the chief priests and Pharisees; and they said unto them, Why did ye not bring Jesus? The officers answered, Never man so spake.

§15 Farewell Discourse of Jesus

Now before the feast of the passover, Jesus knowing that his hour was come that he should depart out of this world unto the Father, having loved his own which were in the world, he loved them unto the end. And he said unto them,

Let not your heart be troubled: ye believe in God, believe also in me. I am the way, and the truth, and the life: no one cometh unto the Father, but by me. Philip saith unto him, Master, shew us the Father, and it sufficeth us. Jesus saith unto him, Have I been so long time with you, and dost thou not know me, Philip? he that hath seen me hath seen the Father; how sayest thou, Shew us the Father? Believest thou not that I am in the Father, and the Father in me? the words that I say unto you I speak not from myself. Believe me that I am in the Father, and the Father in me.

I am the true vine, and my Father is the husbandman. Every branch in me that beareth not fruit, he taketh it away: and every branch that beareth fruit, he pruneth it, that it may bear more fruit. Abide in me, and I in you. As the branch cannot bear fruit of itself, except it abide in the vine; so neither can ye, except ye abide in me. I am the vine, ye are the branches: He that abideth in me, and I in him, the same beareth much fruit: for apart from me ye can do nothing. Herein is my Father glorified, that ye bear much fruit; and so shall ye be my disciples.

Ye shall bear witness of me, because ye have been with me from the beginning. If the world hateth you, ye know that it hath hated me before it hated you. If ye were of the world, the world would love its own: but because ye are not of the world, therefore the world hateth you. Remember the word that I said unto you, A servant is not greater than his master. If they persecuted me, they will also persecute you. But all these things will they do unto you, because they know not him that sent me. If I had not come and spoken unto them, they had not had sin: but now they have no excuse for their sin. He that hateth me hateth my Father also. These things have I spoken unto you, that ye should not be made to stumble. They shall put you out of the synagogues: yea, the hour cometh, that whosoever killeth you shall think that he offereth service unto God. And these things will they do, because they have not known the Father, nor me. But when the Spirit of truth is come, which proceedeth from the Father, he shall bear witness of me. And he, when he is come, will convict the world in respect of sin, and of righteousness, and of judgement.

A little while, and ye behold me no more; and again a little while, and ye shall see me. Some of his disciples therefore said one to another, What is this that he saith unto us, A little while, and ye behold me not; and again a little while, and ye shall see me. We know not what he saith. Jesus perceived that they were desirous to ask him, and he said unto them, Do ye inquire among yourselves concerning this, that I said, A little while, and ye behold me not, and again a little while, and ye shall see me? I will not leave you desolate: I come unto you. Yet a little while, and the world beholdeth me no more; but ye behold me: because I live, ye shall live also. In that day ye shall know that I am

in my Father, and ye in me, and I in you.
He that hath my commandments, and keepeth them, he it is that loveth me: and he that loveth me shall be loved of my Father, and I will love him, and will manifest myself unto him. Judas (not Iscariot) saith unto him, Master, what is come to pass that thou wilt manifest thyself unto us, and not unto the world? Jesus answered and said unto him, If a man love me, he will keep my word: and my Father will love him, and we will come unto him, and make our abode with him.
Even as the Father hath loved me, I also have loved you: abide ye in my love. If ye keep my commandments, ye shall abide in my love; even as I have kept my Father's commandments, and abide in his love. This is my commandment, that ye love one another, even as I have loved you. Greater love hath no man than this, that a man lay down his life for his friends. Ye are my friends, if ye do the things which I command you. A new commandment I give unto you, that ye love one another; even as I have loved you, that ye also love one another. By this shall all men know that ye are my disciples, if ye have love one to another.
If ye love me, ye will keep my commandments. And I will pray the Father, and he shall give you another, that he may be with you for ever, even the Spirit of truth: whom the world cannot receive; for it knoweth him not: ye know him; for he abideth with you, and shall be in you. I have yet many things to say unto you, but ye cannot bear them now. Howbeit when

he, the Spirit of truth, is come, he shall guide you into all the truth. for he shall not speak from himself; but what things soever he shall hear, these shall he speak. He shall take of mine, and shall declare it unto you. All things whatsoever the Father hath are mine: therefore said I, that he taketh of mine, and shall declare it unto you. These things have I spoken unto you, while yet abiding with you. But the Holy Spirit, whom the Father will send, he shall teach you all things.
Behold, the hour cometh, yea, is come, that ye shall be scattered, every man to his own, and shall leave me alone: and yet I am not alone, because the Father is with me. These things have I spoken unto you, that in me ye may have peace. In the world ye have tribulation: but be of good cheer; I have overcome the world. Peace I leave with you; my peace I give unto you: not as the world giveth, give I unto you. Let not your heart be troubled, neither let it be fearful. If ye loved me, ye would have rejoiced, because I go unto the Father: for the Father is greater than I. I will no more speak much with you. That the world may know that I love the Father, and as the Father gave me commandment, even so I do. Arise, let us go hence.

§16 Farewell Prayer of Jesus

These things spake Jesus; and lifting up his eyes to heaven, he said,
Father, the hour is come; glorify thy Son, that the Son may glorify thee. I glorified thee on the earth, having accomplished the work which thou hast given

me to do. I manifested thy name unto the men whom thou gavest me out of the world: thine they were, and thou gavest them to me; and they have kept thy word. Now they know that all things whatsoever thou hast given me are from thee: for the words which thou gavest me I have given unto them; and they received them, and knew of a truth that I came forth from thee, and they believed that thou didst send me.

And now, O Father, I pray for them: I pray not for the world, but for those whom thou hast given me; for they are thine: and all things that are mine are thine, and thine are mine: and I am glorified in them. And I am no more in the world, and these are in the world, and I come to thee.

Holy Father, keep them in thy name which thou hast given me, that they may be one, even as we are. While I was with them, I kept them in thy name which thou hast given me. But now I come to thee. I have given them thy word; and the world hated them, because they are not of the world, even as I am not of the world. I pray not that thou shouldest take them from the world, but that thou shouldest keep them from evil. Sanctify them in the truth: thy word is truth. And for their sakes I consecrate myself, that they themselves also may be dedicated in truth.

Neither for these only do I pray, but for them also that believe on me through their word; that they may all be one; even as thou, Father, art in me, and I in thee, that they also may be in us: that the world may believe that thou didst send me. And the glory which thou hast given me I have given unto them; that they

may be one, even as we are one; I in them, and thou in me, that they may be perfected into one; that the world may know that thou didst send me, and lovedst them, even as thou lovedst me.
O righteous Father, the world knew thee not, but I knew thee; and these knew that thou didst send me; and I made known unto them thy name, that the love wherewith thou lovedst me may be in them, and I in them.

§ 17 Jesus and Pilate

When Jesus had spoken these words, he went forth with his disciples over the brook Kidron, where was a garden, into the which he entered, himself and his disciples. Now Judas also, which betrayed him, knew the place: for Jesus oft-times resorted thither with his disciples. Judas then, having received the band of soldiers, and officers from the chief priests and the Pharisees, cometh thither with lanterns and torches and weapons. So the band and the chief captain, and the officers of the Jews, seized Jesus and bound him, and led him to Annas first; for he was father in law to Caiaphas, which was high priest that year. Annas sent him bound unto Caiaphas the high priest. They lead Jesus from Caiaphas into the palace.
Pilate entered into the palace, and called Jesus, and said unto him, Art thou the King of the Jews? Jesus answered, Sayest thou this of thyself, or did others tell it thee concerning me? Pilate answered, Am I a Jew? Thine own nation and the chief priests delivered thee unto me: what hast thou done? Jesus answered, My

kingdom is not of this world: if my kingdom were of this world, then would my servants fight, that I should not be delivered to the Jews: but now is my kingdom not from hence. Pilate therefore said unto him, Art thou a king then? Jesus answered, Thou sayest that I am a king. To this end have I been born, and to this end am I come into the world, that I should bear witness unto the truth. Every one that is of the truth heareth my voice. Pilate saith unto him, What is truth?

EPILOGUE

EPILOGUE ✝ ✝ ✝ ✝

At the end of the study one comes inevitably to the conclusion that it is precisely at that point where the individual most inexorably faces an ultimate decision, where the elemental tension between God and man is most acutely felt, and where at the same time the gulf between God and man is most inwardly and most completely bridged, without any mediation of human doctrines or institutions, that the essential nature of the Founder is most vitally and potently apprehended."

HAND-SET in Foundry Garam nd type by Arthur and Edna Rushmore at the Golden Hind Press in Madison New Jersey MCMXXXV

STUDIES IN
JESUS AS TEACHER

Books by

H. B. SHARMAN

JESUS AS TEACHER
RECORDS OF THE LIFE OF JESUS
SON OF MAN AND KINGDOM OF GOD
STUDIES IN THE RECORDS
PAUL AS EXPERIENT
Harper and Brothers

TEACHING OF JESUS ABOUT THE FUTURE
University of Chicago Press

JESUS IN THE RECORDS
Association Press

STUDIES IN JESUS AS TEACHER

By

Henry Burton Sharman Ph D

HARPER & BROTHERS PUBLISHERS

New York and London

STUDIES IN JESUS AS TEACHER

Printed in the United States of America

CONTENTS

PROLOGUE

Familiarity with the wording probably makes more against the sound understanding and worthy evaluation of the teaching of Jesus than does any other factor. Because one has throughout life frequently heard, and often independently read, the sayings of Jesus, generally under conditions making slight demand for close attention, and even less call for serious consideration, the teaching has become a body of words that have lost the power to arrest and command the activity of the mind and the response of the spirit.

Perhaps nothing can contribute more toward penetrating this deadening familiarity than to be confronted by questions, on the material, fashioned by other minds, which seek to get beneath the surface of the narrative or teaching. That is the conviction which has determined the method and form of these *Studies*.

Information is not the primary need of the serious student of the deeds and words of Jesus. Masses of information are available; they could be assembled and presented. But they would contribute nothing toward the breakdown of that barrier of familiarity which leaves one still standing outside the pale of actual apprehension. Better not to understand something that information could clarify than thus to understand much that is not notably worth understanding.

Familiarity with the wording, and Information about secondary matters, both stand in the way of the direct application of the mind to the meaning of the thought and to its evaluation. And when the information has, as its major interest, the problem of historicity, the edge of penetration into meanings, as distinguished from source, is likely to be seriously dulled. It tends to make the value of expressed thought seem wholly dependent upon the decision as to who spoke the thought rather than upon its inherent significance, or lack of significance, whatever its source.

It should not be supposed that the Questions which make up these *Studies* stand on an even level of difficulty and of consequent worth for the student. Some of them may be answered with ease by any attentive reader of the text on which they are based. It may even be wondered at times why questions of such simplicity are considered worth asking. But one may not wisely then abandon the study, for probably it is true that, in the main, the questions will be found to demand close attention, and often prolonged thought, before the text yields the satisfying answer.

These *Studies* are adapted for use by the individual in the endeavor to understand the thought. They do not presuppose outside reading nor group thought. But they are so fashioned that they may be made the basis for subsequent discussion as a part of that group process of thorough thought together which is calculated to yield very much more than can ever be had by the isolated efforts of any individual.

The problem of Leadership for group study is greatly reduced when the function of the Leader is no longer regarded as the imparting of information, but rather as the confrontation of others with questions for which the answers are discoverable in the text under consideration. And when the leader assumes the attitude that a leader's own answers to the questions are not usually more likely to be valuable or dependable than are those reached by group discussion, the function of the leader becomes simply that of holding the mind of the group to the limits of the issues set by the questions, and determining when discussion has reached the end of being really profitable.

Because of the notable rewards of group discussion when held within the bounds set by some definite text, it is to be hoped that there will be wide recognition of the fact that, with the questions which make up these *Studies* in the possession of every member of a group, hesitation need not be felt because of the fact that no person with special equipment of knowledge or experience is available for leadership. The loyal following of these questions in a group, one after another in their own order, giving that minimum of time which the simplicity of some of them suggest and that maximum of time which the difficulty of others of them will demand, reduces the responsibility of the Leader to that level which brings it within average capacity.

The gravest danger that besets group discussion is the ever-active tendency to range beyond the limits naturally set by the content of the text that is directly under consideration. Interchange of opinion may speedily lose all of its notable inherent values and become simply futile wandering unless some control is exercised over its direction; therein consists the primary and all-important function of the Leader—not in imparting relatively valueless information nor in telling others what they ought to think.

Some of the sayings attributed to Jesus seem to be statements of considerable profundity. In a Foundation Lecture at Cambridge University on *The Name and Nature of Poetry*, the assertion was ventured, naturally quite incidentally, about one of the sayings of Jesus: "That is the most important truth which has ever been uttered, and the greatest discovery ever made." If this is not a mistaken judgment, then something more than superficial and hurried heed will be called for in the serious study of the Teaching of Jesus.

PROCESSES OF GROUP THINKING

PROCESSES OF GROUP THINKING

I Conditions for Group Thinking

II Suggestions to Group Members

III Suggestions to Group Leaders

- A Management of Discussion
- B Introduction to the Study
- C Attitude of the Leader
- D Some General Principles
- E Dealing with Members
- F Some Specific Situations
- G Goal in these *Studies*

PROCESSES OF GROUP THINKING

by L. Earl Willmott, M.A.

I *Conditions for Group Thinking*

Group thinking is the process by which a group arrives at an understanding or a decision. Group thinking produces something that members individually cannot produce—it creates a group idea that may be better than the best individual idea or all the individual ideas added together. The means by which this group thinking is carried on is the method of discussion. Discussion differs from argument and debate. An argument takes place when minds are already made up and each side has the desire to convince its opponents of its soundness. A debate is a controversy around one proposed solution where each side desires to convince the hearers that it is right. A discussion is the process whereby a group of individuals seek together for conviction as to the best solution to some problem, and where no one is sure beforehand what the outcome of his own or the group's thinking will be.

It is easy for a group to talk, but that does not necessarily mean that there is group thinking. It is difficult for a group to do real thinking. There are certain conditions which make possible or facilitate group thinking:

1. Each member of the group must put all he has into the common stock—sharing, co-operating, with that attitude of open searching which, when it meets something in opposition to a held viewpoint, does not say, "Now, this is awkward; how can I refute it?" but which says, "This is interesting; let us give it full weight and see its possibilities."

2. The group must adopt some procedure, a process of thinking in orderly sequence, more or less specifically and consciously followed according to circumstances.

3. There must be a leader to keep the group going along together, to encourage sharing, to pass on from point to point, to keep the group aware of the ground covered and the road

they are travelling. He starts things, keeps them going, and winds them up, but does not do them. He need not be an expert on the subject under discussion, but he should know in general all the points that are likely to arise during the discussion. As the size of the group increases, the leader's ability to lead discussion must increase greatly.

4. The group should feel its corporateness and there should be a sense of mutuality and fellowship. For the most effective group thinking, the members should be able to see each others' faces: they should be held into a group by physical means, such as a table around which they can sit, or placed comfortably and informally around a small room.

5. The group should be between six and fifteen or thereabouts in numbers. That is not to say that one cannot have group discussion in a group of fifty or five hundred; but very quickly as the numbers increase above fifteen or twenty the chance for every one to participate diminishes, until there may be just a small minority taking part and the rest more or less active listeners. Experience shows that for most of us there is a definite psychological limit to the number of persons with whom we can share our best thinking in a personal and useful way. This limit is soon reached when more than fifteen get together. Beyond this number, fellowship is difficult to cultivate, and each member's sense of direct, personal responsibility for the group's efficiency begins to vanish. Generally speaking, it would be better to have several smaller groups with relatively inexperienced leaders than one over-large group with an able leader.

Streeter of Oxford University has written thus of Group Thinking:

"Discovery comes whenever trains of thought or pieces of information originally separate are seen to illuminate and explain each other. But when the things requiring to be brought together exist in different minds, this fusion is made harder or easier in exact proportion to the degree of sympathy and the range of contact between these minds.

"The maximum possibilities of the fusion of such different strains is reached when there is personal as well as intellectual understanding, and where there is an overmastering passion for truth which makes each willing to put all he has into the common stock, to hold back no half-formed thought as foolish or immature, and to defend no position once taken up merely from respect to interest or conservatism.

"Such co-operation is not always an easy thing to compass; but when it exists, persons of quite modest gifts and moderate experience can do, relatively to their capacity, great things."

II *Suggestions to Group Members*

Maintain an attitude of *searching* for a solution. You are not trying to convince anyone of an opinion—you are trying to find the best answer.

Never undertake to say to the group what another member of the group means by what he has stated.

Listen to learn. Do not be thinking up what to say next while another is speaking and so miss his contribution.

Avoid the use of stereotyped phraseology. Clothe thought in different and fresh words. Strive for versatility in terminology.

Participate. Contribute your idea. Do not hold back an idea because it seems to you incomplete—it may be just the idea that the group needs in order to move ahead. Often an indifferent contribution leads to productive thinking by the group.

Do not allow anything permanently to pass unchallenged which makes you rebellious.

Say what you really think. Do not speak to please anyone. Be honest.

Talk to the point. Do not start off on a different track, unless you feel sure that doing so will throw light on the problem.

Endeavor to hold your preconceptions in abeyance. Be on guard against the influence of your own bias. This will prove to be a difficult discipline but highly rewarding.

Talk briefly. Say what you have to say and stop. Give the other members as much chance to talk as you have had. Sometimes refrain from speaking, to encourage the more hesitant.

Be on the lookout for evidence that will change your mind. Do not hesitate to say that you have changed your mind, if you have. You will command more respect from the group for that than by sticking to an opinion expressed earlier that begins to look untenable to the group.

Be sympathetic toward the opinion of another *as opinion.* If you think it in error, be eager to follow it until it corrects itself, rather than try yourself to correct it directly and promptly.

It is legitimate for one member of the group to ask another

member to restate his position when that position has not been made clear to everybody. But it is dubious practice to attempt to undermine by asking concerning the processes by which the position was reached. Better to make one's own independent contribution, stating its grounds.

III *Suggestions to Group Leaders*

A *Management of Discussion*

The discussion leader exists to help the group mobilize its own thought resources and direct these to the attack on the problem at hand.

Have a definite outline and procedure in mind (or on paper) and follow it, but not so rigidly as to lose a promising lead. Think through the procedure, the problems and issues that are likely to call for discussion.

Be ready with questions to meet the developing interest of the group, and so reduce to a minimum the necessity for phrasing questions on the spur of the moment. Make it a fixed rule to avoid altogether, and at all times, the use of any question which can be answered by the word "Yes" or by the word "No." Nothing is more likely to stifle thought, and particularly expression of thought, than falling into the habit of asking, even occasionally, Yes-No questions.

Be persistent in holding the group to the point; see that they know what they are talking about—but do not guide the discussion to any prior or externally chosen end.

Move the discussion along; see that the thinking keeps progressing. When "everything has been said," or a certain point has been sufficiently covered in view of the time available, lead the group on to the next point. On the other hand, there may be cases in which the group should be held from moving along too fast, for example, from making a hasty decision before all the facts are clearly seen.

From time to time make summaries: indicate the trend of discussion, the agreements reached, the significant differences of opinion—lest the woods be missed for the trees. This will bring to many members surer satisfaction that results have been reached, and will give them something more definite to take away as an outcome of the discussion. Give the group the chance to criticize or amend your summary.

B *Introduction to the Study*

Start the work with the group by a plain statement that the prime necessity for progress as a group is that there shall be always absolute frankness and outspokenness of opinion.

From the outset, encourage the group not to think of the leader as knowing so much more than the group that the members hesitate to venture their own opinions.

The members of the group should be informed that the leader does not necessarily express his evaluation of the contributions made by members. His silence must not be regarded as either condemnation or commendation. Requests by him for the views of others may properly and profitably be made even after what he thinks is the sound view has already been expressed and not opposed.

The leader should make it clear to the group that he is quite as liable as are others to misunderstand statements of group members, and that he welcomes criticisms, challenges, and suggestions as to his methods and attitudes.

The members of a group should understand, at the beginning of their work together, that their responses to questions, from whatever source, should be made to the group as a whole and not directed toward the leader or the questioner.

C *Attitude of the Leader*

It is even more essential for the leader to hold all preconceptions in abeyance than for the group members. Until he can free himself from the control of his prejudgments, no person should ever undertake to lead a group in the co-operative search for truth. That search is a task of discovery for the leader as well as for the group members.

The leader is concerned not alone with the majority of the group but with the exploration of any significant point to the satisfaction of every member, particularly those members who check the group on its easy understandings and challenge them.

The leader should not make obvious at once by his attitude what his own reaction is to the contribution of any member. That may tend to inhibit rather than to encourage additional discussion.

The leader should recognize that sole responsibility for the successful functioning of the group does not rest upon him. Any acceptance of leadership that results in strain or tenseness in action is evidence that the leader has improperly conceived his place in the group.

Encourage all possible points-of-view. It may be difficult for the leader to feel quite impartial, but he should bear in mind that no point-of-view will be reached and subsequently held with confidence if any facts or viewpoints in opposition are withheld or repressed during the discussion. Let him not be afraid of any possible outcome; nor weight the discussion toward predetermined conclusions (The Socratic method, however good for some things, is not the method of Group Thinking).

It is not necessary to acknowledge every contribution, nor to be the center through which every contribution must pass, nor to repeat or summarize what others have said. In this way one will probably spoil the group interaction and make it a member-leader relationship, as well as using valuable time.

Be fearful about forcing your own opinions. Never argue with a member. Do not break in on the discussion which seems to be going against your opinion—*trust the group.* Do not keep the group from deciding on what you think is wrong. See that all the facts and viewpoints have been brought out.

Hesitate to talk much. The leader's task is to get expression from as many of the group as possible. His primary function is to face the group with questions—not to give the answers to questions nor to talk.

Avoid arousing any irritation toward the leader. Use consideration, tolerance, and tact.

Set a limit to your criticism or suggestion as to the group's methods in discussion. The group can often learn by experience better than by being told.

While a leader might sometimes step out of leadership for a moment while he contributes some information or an opinion, in general it is better to put the burden on the group.

Make no decision with which you think the group would not agree, such as shutting off a member who seems to be talking too long or off the point. Sense the group's intention and attitude toward the talker.

D *Some General Principles*

Only occasionally is it advisable to repeat or reformulate a contribution. It may be helpful at times, when the point has not been made clear to all, or to help the group re-think a significant contribution.

Sometimes special tasks may be delegated to members—making notes of things to be looked up, giving information called for at previous meetings, even making summaries covering main points of the discussion.

If there is a distinct difference of opinion in the group—a conflict—be sure that neither side feels that it has been unfairly treated. See that all significant aspects of both sides have been adequately presented.

Never be afraid of silence. Silence may be sterile, but it may indicate a need for careful thought. If you are sure the question is understood, give the group plenty of time to think.

Be aware of the possibility that the apparent differences of opinion among members may be because they are using the same word with different meanings. Be sure that the group has common definitions for important terms.

Allow no one member of a group to tell another member what that other member has thought or what he means by what he has just expressed as his thought.

It is unfortunate when the group is made to feel any sense of drive or hurry. Group discussion should always be leisurely—not desultory or wandering but also not hastened or tense.

It is not necessary for the group to have reached agreement in order for the time to have arrived for the discussion to move forward. Group conclusions as an outcome are less important than that the process of discussion be open-minded, thorough, frank, and outspoken.

Hold the attention of the group to the material or theme directly under consideration. Do not permit ranging to other areas of thought.

Personal remarks and jokes are not to be discouraged; humor when quite spontaneous is one of the greatest solvents of egotism and a well-spring of fellowship and mutual understanding.

E *Dealing with Members*

Be sure that the members of the group know one another. Spend enough time at the beginning to get acquainted.

Keep using names of members when referring to anyone or his contribution to the thinking. This is especially important if the group is just beginning to know one another. If you do not know a name, find out.

Enlist as many members of the group in the discussion as possible, and encourage them to begin as early as possible—anyone contributing thereby gives hostage to later interest and participation. But be slow to call on any member—voluntary contribution is better than solicited.

Sometimes one can do much between meetings by talking with members: to find out what may be standing in the way of their profiting by the discussion; or to encourage one who feels that he was "sat on"; or to develop the thinking of one who seems lost; or to find some knowledge or experience that was not contributed to the group.

Educate the members of the group to discuss—to function in group thinking. It is the responsibility of the leader to see that they have before them not only the suggestions give in Section II above, but also any other hints that the experience of the leader brings to his mind.

F *Some Specific Situations*

If someone is running on and on, politely and good-humoredly interrupt: "I'm afraid that you are perhaps giving us more than we can handle. Your main point was . . . (summarize it)." Or, "You are making some engaging suggestions; would it not be helpful now to get the thinking of other members?"

If someone is giving a too-long personal experience to illustrate his point, interrupt as soon as his point is clear to you, with some such statement as: "If I understand you, you are telling us that . . . (summarize his point)."

If the group is examining a situation that is personal, and charged with emotion exhibited in contentious arguments, carry on the discussion in the third person by asking: "Why do some people think . . .?," thus introducing an opinion on some other side (making sure that it is not regarded as your opinion).

If the group is getting so emotionally stirred that rational thinking is impaired: first, remain calm and objective; second, carry the thought yourself—not dodging the issue but meeting it even more directly than the group has been doing—by summarizing what has been said and advancing new considerations; and third, if anyone insists on speaking, draw the remarks to yourself by asking the group to listen with you in an effort to understand his point-of-view.

If a member begins to get off the track and becomes perhaps wordy, be firm as well as polite. "Perhaps we would better not explore any farther in that direction" or, "I'm doubtful whether that will be any significant help to the point."

If any two members start talking together while someone else is speaking, perhaps temporarily interrupting say to one of them, "Would you mind holding that thought until we have all heard what the speaker is saying and then contribute your thought to the whole group?"

If there seems to be a deadlock, or the thinking has lagged, suggest a short break in the discussion. During the recess the members will talk freely and spontaneously with each other and, when the group reconvenes, the discussion will likely move forward more smoothly and freely.

If any member of the group holds to some value or principle with a fixed attitude, as something that "cannot be compromised," do not let the group try to break down his resistance, but draw attention to the need of understanding different people's tests for truth. It might be helpful, on occasion, to direct the discussion toward finding out the genesis of strongly held opinions, attitudes, and prejudices.

G *Goal in these Studies*

The ultimate goal in these *Studies* is a clear perception of the Way of Life as understood and taught by Jesus, rather than a meticulous examination of the whole body of material from every angle. That the group reach the former rather than do the latter is to be regarded as the major responsibility of the Leader.

BOOK I

THE RECORD OF MATTHEW MARK AND LUKE

BOOK I

THE RECORD OF MATTHEW MARK AND LUKE

BOOK I

THE RECORD OF MATTHEW MARK AND LUKE

CHAPTER I

STATEMENTS ABOUT ORIGINS

§1 *Origin of the Records*

1 What was the dominant impression about his book that the author of this foreword wished to convey?

2 What does he reveal as to the sources of information available to him?

3 In what degree did he have access to eyewitnesses of the events he records?

4 What was the likelihood as to his treatment of those written narratives which he asserts were already in existence before he began his work?

5 In the event that one could subsequently prove that the author made some reports that lack accuracy, what would be the legitimate influence on one's attitude toward his material?

6 If it could be proven that some significant sayings attributed to Jesus by the author did not actually originate with him but came from a) older Jewish sources, or b) were the product of the early Christian community, what evaluation should one put upon such sayings?

7 In what measure is the truth and value of any teaching dependent upon the source from which it comes?

8 "All things accurately" and "know the certainty": if the authors of the original books about Jesus were proven, as to their narrative portions, to be not always "accurate", and if the attempted attainment of historical "certainty" through their accounts were shown to be illusory, what effect would that justifiably have upon one's estimate of the ultimate worth of the teaching attributed by them to Jesus?

§2 *Birth of Jesus at Bethlehem*

"There went out a decree from Caesar Augustus": this is an

indication that, in the time of Jesus, Palestine was one part of what empire?

§3 *The Dedication at Jerusalem*

1 "His name was called Jesus": by what name is he now most generally called? b) What justification is there for calling him by any name other than that given him at his dedication?

2 When he is referred to as "Jesus Christ", what part is name and what part is title? b) When one goes beyond the name of a person and attaches a title to a person, one has already done what, relative to that person?

3 The word "Messiah" in Hebrew, "Christos" in Greek, "Christus" in Latin, and "Christ" in English, all mean etymologically what? For some knowledge of the mode of functioning that was associated with the expected "Messiah" of the Jews in the time of Jesus, consideration should be given at the outset to

Political Messianism

1 "The Lord God shall give unto him the throne of his father David: and he shall reign over the house of Jacob for ever" (Page 145): from which statement it is to be deduced that his work will be of what nature?

2 In view of the context, the phrases "for ever" and "no end" are intended to refer a) to the reign of the individual? or b) to the reign of the dynasty established by the individual? or c) to what?

3 "He shall be called the Son of the Most High": consequently it may be legitimate to consider that the phrase "Son of the Most High" as a title may be equated with what single English word from the Hebrew language?

4 "Son of the Most High": it would be congenial to Hebrew religious thought to take "Son" as bearing what sense?

5 "Looking for the redemption of Jerusalem": when the "consolation" of Israel and the "redemption" of Jerusalem were high hopes held by the Jewish people in the time of Jesus, they meant by the "redemption" of Jerusalem definitely what?

6 "Where should the Christ be born?": born to function after what manner as the Christ, judging from the associated question in the line that precedes?

7 "Out of thee shall come forth a governor": from which it is to be deduced that the career of the Christ is to take what form of activity?

8 "Redemption for his people" . . . "salvation for us" . . . "salvation from our enemies" . . . "delivered out of the hand of our enemies": the work of the Christ was thought of in such form by the contemporaries of Jesus that the meaning of "redemption" and "salvation" at the hands of the Christ was concretely what?

9 "Hosanna to the son of David!" . . . "Hosanna in the highest!": these reputed greetings are called forth by the person so acclaimed because it is believed that he is destined to accomplish for the people of Israel what specific ends?

10 "Art thou the Christ, the Son of the Blessed?" . . . "He says that he himself is Christ a king" . . . "Art thou the King of the Jews?": from which it is evident that for the contemporaries of Jesus the term "Christ" was to be equated with what other term?

11 "THIS IS JESUS THE KING OF THE JEWS": Jesus was executed under the charge that he claimed to be the Christ and as such was making the assertion that he bore what relation to the Jewish people?

12 What historical justification is there for adding the title "Christ" to the name "Jesus", in view of the contemporary Jewish content for the term "Christ"?

§4 *The Return to Nazareth*

"They returned into Galilee": the absence of Joseph and Mary from their own province and city is reported to have been occasioned by what event?

§5 *The Youth of Jesus*

What should one choose as the most accurate and adequate single word to describe or define the youth of Jesus?

§6 *Jesus as Student*

1 How account for the eager and absorbed interest of Jesus, at the age of twelve, in the discussions of the Jewish teachers?

b) What was probably the subject matter of their discussions?

2 What was the nature of the knowledge or insight displayed by Jesus on this occasion in his relations with the teachers?

3 What single word best describes the reaction of Jesus to the questioning of him by his parents?

4 When Jesus referred to the temple as "my Father's house", what content for his mind would the term "Father" hold, assuming that it was a term occasionally used for God by Jewish people?

5 If one were to assume that the term "Father" as a mode of designation for God was altogether original with Jesus, what would reasonably be the maximum content for the expression?

6 How state succinctly what one may learn about Jesus as a youth from this episode in Jerusalem?

§7 *Development of Jesus*

Judging from the statement about the first twelve years of his life (Section 5) and the summary of the subsequent eighteen years (Section 7), how characterize the nature and mode of those thirty years which preceded the public activity of Jesus?

CHAPTER II

ACTIVITY OF JOHN AND ITS RELATION TO JESUS

§8 *Statement of the Work of John*

1 According to the criticism voiced by John against the religious authorities of his day, on what did they base their supposed acceptance by God?

2 What did John propose as his substitute for the basis that prevailed in the minds of the religious authorities?

3 What outlook upon the future did John hold as intimated by "the wrath to come" and "hewn down and cast into the fire"?

4 What evaluation should be placed on each of the several reported ethical norms of John?

5 How state otherwise the most general of the expressed ethical norms of John?

6 "Whether haply he were the Christ": what were the qualities possessed and manifest by John that suggested to "the people who were in expectation" that possibly John might be the anticipated Christ?

7 "Hewn down and cast into the fire" . . . "baptize you with fire" . . . "burn up with unquenchable fire": from these terms about the activity of the Christ used by John, how characterize his conception of the essential function of the Christ?

8 "There cometh he that is mightier": cometh when? b) What evidence is there as to the time when John thought the Christ would appear for the accomplishing of his work? c) What evidence is there here that John thought of Jesus as the Christ?

9 What was the influence that led John to contrast his own mode of activity with that which he conceived to be the mode of the Christ?

10 Since the mode of functioning of the Christ, as set forth by John, has in it nothing of political activity against Rome, but is rather the execution of drastic judgment upon the unrighteous among the Jewish people, it becomes apparent that more than one form of Messianism prevailed in the time of

Jesus. The views of John the Baptist about the work of the Coming One find their parallelism in

Apocalyptic Messianism

1 In the succession of passages descriptive of Apocalyptic Messianism (Pages 147-149), it is discoverable that the title to be borne by the Coming One is in form a phrase rather than a single word as in Political Messianism: what is that phrase as determined by a complete reading of all the passages?

2 Whose kingdom is the kingdom that is to be realized on the occasion of the coming of the Son of man at some future time?

3 From a study of all the passages on pages 147-149, what conclusion should be reached as to the time set a) for the realization of the kingdom of God, and b) for the coming of the Son of man?

4 What is the difference, if any, between the realization of the kingdom of God and the coming of the Son of man?

5 What is represented as being the primary function of the Son of man and those acting with him on the occasion of the coming of the Son of man at the end of the world?

6 What is the relation between the function here associated with the coming of the Son of man and that assigned to the Christ by John the Baptist? b) Both of them are vivid descriptions of what form of contemporary Messianism?

§9 *Baptism of Jesus by John*

1 What qualities among those displayed by John may be supposed to have made strong enough appeal to Jesus to lead him to ally himself with the movement of John?

2 What elements in the situation may have created hesitancy on the part of Jesus toward committing himself to the implications of definite association with John?

3 How account for the chosen act of relationship with John having resulted for Jesus in a deepened sense of the presence of God and the conviction of complete approval by and fellowship with God?

4 Who was the most highly determinative factor in the experience of Jesus on the occasion of his baptism—John, or Jesus, or God?

5 In what respect was Jesus different after his baptism expe-

rience than he had been before that experience had followed upon his alliance with John?

6 "This day have I begotten thee": arbitrarily? fortuitously? for some causal reason? If for some reason, for what reason?

§10 *Withdrawal of Jesus to the Wilderness*

1 Why should Jesus have had to consider seriously, in the period following his baptism, the question of his personal relation to direct political rule? b) What was the contemporary situation which prompted that as an immediate and vital issue for anybody contemplating leadership?

2 "If thou art": then expect what from God in the event of wilful exposure to extreme physical danger? or when brought by historical developments into threatening conflicts? What concept about "the Son of God" is implicit within this second of the problems faced?

3 Turning a stone into a loaf may be regarded as a strikingly vivid way of portraying what state of economic condition? b) According to Hebrew tradition (Genesis 3:17-19), why was man condemned to the necessity of working hard for his bread? c) Under what circumstances therefore might mankind expect bread without labor? d) What concept about "the Son of God" is implicit within this third of the problems faced?

4 In view of the essential content of the several issues faced and decided on this occasion, what should be regarded as the meaning here of the phrase "the Son of God"?

5 How account for the fact that Jesus had not considered and settled the problems at issue during this retirement before reaching this stage of his development? b) How did it come about that Jesus was now confronted by these major problems?

6 What evidence can be found within the account that Jesus had any strong impulse to go in any direction that he considered to be wrong?

7 How state, in general terms, what it was that engaged the mind of Jesus during this period of withdrawal subsequent to his baptism?

CHAPTER III

BEGINNINGS OF THE PUBLIC ACTIVITY OF JESUS

§11 *General Statement of the Work of Jesus*

Judging from this general statement set at the forefront of the activity of Jesus, what did he regard as the proper fundamental mode of his personal functioning on behalf of his aims?

§12 *Jesus Teaches at Nazareth*

1 In the book of the Prophet Isaiah (Isaiah 61:1-2), to whom does Isaiah refer by "me" in the phrases "upon me" . . . "anointed me" . . . "sent me" when spoken?

2 What was the evident political state of those addressed by Isaiah as it may be deduced from the study of the verse that follows (Isaiah 61:4)?

3 When had the confident hope of Isaiah as expressed in this outlook upon the future of his people had its substantial realization?

4 "Anointed to preach" . . . "sent to proclaim": Isaiah expresses in these words what form of sense of vocation?

5 If the passage from Isaiah that was read by Jesus on that occasion be regarded as the basis of his discourse, what may one consider as the theme within it which Jesus would most naturally develop into a talk?

6 What was the total reaction of the hearers to the message wrought out by Jesus from the Isaian passage?

7 In what measure may it be supposed that Jesus talked explicitly about himself on this occasion?

8 "Is not this Joseph's son?": what had Jesus become that made him more than Joseph's son? b) How had this been attained?

§13 *Jesus Teaches at Capernaum*

1 "He taught them as having authority": wherein did the impression of authority created by Jesus differ from the authority inherent with the scribes?

2 What was the source of the "authority" a) of the scribes, and b) of Jesus?

§14 *Jesus and Mental Cases*

1 "Them that were possessed with devils": what terms are used at the present time to describe the type of affliction meant here?

2 What is the most potent form of influence for dealing with persons thus afflicted?

3 "They believed that he was the Christ": what titles did they use for Jesus as being synonyms for the term Christ?

4 "Art thou come to torment us? Art thou come to destroy us?": what conception of the work of the Christ finds expression in these outcries of those who were regarded as possessed by demons?

5 "We know thee who thou art": how account for the fact that this element in the populace was most outspoken in early and definite appraisal of Jesus as the Christ?

6 "Jesus suffered them not to speak": what various alternative views may be advanced in explanation of the fact that Jesus sought to suppress declarations to the effect that he was the Christ?

§15 *Jesus Teaches by the Lake*

From this narrative one may consider that Jesus regarded what as the major form of his personal functioning?

§16 *Jesus Wins Fisherman Followers*

1 What motive may reasonably be attributed to Jesus for proposing that they fish subsequent to his use of their boat?

2 "I am a sinful man, O Master": by what influence from Jesus was that conviction produced within Simon Peter?

3 "From henceforth thou shalt catch men": is this to be regarded as a command, or as an invitation, or as an intimation, or what?

§17 *Jesus Teaches Throughout Galilee*

"For to this end came I forth": what does the evidence indicate as to what Jesus regarded as the central and essential mode of his functioning for the achievement of his life purposes?

CHAPTER IV

DEVELOPMENT OF OPPOSITION TO JESUS

§18 *Criticism of Free Forgiveness for Sin*

1 What was the prevailing Jewish conception, in the time of Jesus, as to the relationship between disease and sin?

2 "Son, thy sins are forgiven": what contribution could this declaration make toward the achievement of the end for which the palsied man had been brought into the presence of Jesus?

3 "Who can forgive sins but one, even God?": since obviously God could not directly and audibly pronounce absolution for sins, what was the process within the Jewish law by which sin could be propitiated and its forgiveness assured?

4 What declaration was Jesus implicitly making about the contemporary process relative to forgiveness when he acted as he did in this case?

5 On what original bases of his own about man and sin and God and forgiveness must Jesus have been functioning when he spoke to the paralytic as he did without any sense of therein being blasphemous?

6 What did Jesus actually do for the sick of the palsy other than to assure him that his sins were forgiven?

§19 *Criticism for Association with Sinners*

1 What was the motivation that led Jesus into relationship with classes in the community that were socially outcast?

2 What did Jesus think could be accomplished by ignoring the usual bounds of social and religious fellowship?

3 What conception of God and of religion was inherent in the position taken by Jesus on this occasion?

4 "I desire mercy, and not sacrifice": establish the connection between the intention of this saying and the contemporary situation as Jesus observed it in human relationships.

5 "I desire mercy, and not sacrifice": what are the implications of this saying in its larger bearing upon the religious system of the time of Jesus?

§20 *Criticism of Attitude toward Fasting*

1 What evidence, if any, can be advanced, and what is the value of that evidence, in favor of thinking that by the phrase "the bridegroom" Jesus intends to refer to himself?

2 If the reference in "the bridegroom" be regarded as not being personal, why is this figure chosen as the symbol for the truth conveyed?

3 Without the use of the marriage reference, but rather in the abstract form of a general principle, state the position of Jesus relative to the practice of fasting as here set forth by him.

4 By what process may it be supposed that Jesus arrived at his distinctive position relative to fasting?

§21 *Criticism for Working on the Sabbath*

1 "Did ye never read what David did?": what principle of action governed the practice of David on the occasion narrated here? What bearing does that have on sabbath observance?

2 "Have ye not read in the law?": inherent in the practice of the priests was what principle of license bearing upon the sabbath?

3 Having drawn instances from sacred history to suggest his underlying thought, Jesus passes to the enunciation of that thought in abstract form—"The sabbath was made for man, and not man for the sabbath": that being so, what should determine the actual practice of man in his conduct on the sabbath?

4 In what measure is the principle here enunciated by Jesus relative to the sabbath valid for other religious and secular institutions in his age and in our own time?

5 What may be regarded as the genesis of the thought of Jesus relative to the validity of contemporary religious practices and institutions?

§22 *Culmination of Criticism of Jesus*

1 "They took counsel against Jesus, how they might destroy him": arrange, in the order of their apparent seriousness for the religious contemporaries of Jesus, the four points of conflict here recorded as arising between him and them.

2 From which of the four controversies can most be learned

that has vital bearing upon religious thought and practice in our own day?

§23 *Attitude of Jesus toward Criticism*

1 Taking these parables as the source for a judgment, how did Jesus conceive of his teaching in relation to contemporary religious thought?

2 What apparently is destined to be the outcome of any attempt to interpret the teaching of Jesus within the framework of the mode of thinking about religion which was prevalent among his own people in his day?

3 What bearing do these parables have upon the conviction that Jesus as a teacher necessarily must have been "the child of his own generation" in all of his fundamental moral and religious ideals and conceptions about past, present, and future?

4 Judging by the final parable on this occasion, what was the nature of the reception that Jesus expected would be given to his own religious positions?

CHAPTER V

DEFINITION OF STANDARDS OF RIGHTEOUSNESS BY JESUS

§24 *Widespread Fame of Jesus*

1 "Thou art the Son of God": what would be another form of expressing the estimate of Jesus intended by these words from these highly susceptible elements of the populace?

2 "Jesus charged them much": what may one reasonably surmise was the reason why Jesus used such repeated precautions against the spread of these estimates of himself?

§25 *Appointment of Twelve Associates*

What purposes had Jesus in mind for associating a group of men thus closely with himself?

§26 *Discourse on Standards of Righteousness*

1 Judging from the salutation to the disciples with which the discourse opens, from what classes of the community were the disciples of Jesus mainly drawn? b) How account for that fact?

2 Wherein did the blessedness of the early disciples of Jesus consist?

3 "Ye are the salt of the earth": what contemporary group had always considered themselves most eminently worthy of being estimated as the salt of the earth?

4 "Ye are the light of the world": of the officially religious groups in the time of Jesus, what one was, by virtue of its vocation, regarded by itself and by others as the light of the world?

5 "Think not that I came to destroy the law or the prophets": what groups among the Jewish people had been advancing the charge against Jesus that he was a destroyer? b) What were some of the major points on which criticism had been strongly expressed?

6 "The righteousness of the scribes and Pharisees": its

norms were derived from what sources? b) Whence did Jesus derive his own norms?

7 From the age-long established condemnation of the overt act ("kill"), Jesus moves to a position prior to external conduct and pronounces condemnation upon the actually potential genesis ("anger") of the overt act: but how may man control at the genetic point, that is, how may man avoid becoming "angry" when provocation is strong?

8 Against the act ("kill") there stand state laws and penalties; against the impulse ("anger") there stands what penalty?

9 "Then come and offer thy gift": prior to the possibility of any really acceptable relationship with God, what fundamental condition must be fulfiled by man?

10 What evaluation does Jesus place upon the overcoming of physical lust, judging from the drastic nature of his figurative precautions ("eye" and "hand") against its passing into control?

11 Since physical lust naturally thrusts itself upon the consciousness whether or not it is welcome or encouraged by the lustful look, by what process can it be subjected to commendable control?

12 "Swear not at all": what is the inherent implication about one's ordinary statements, not made under oath, that is resident in the practice of the taking of an oath?

13 To what does the practice of the administration of oaths, that is, of calling upon God as attestation of the truth of one's assertions, inevitably lead relative to the standing of those of one's statements that are not so attested, and consequently upon one's attitude toward telling the truth under all circumstances?

14 What is it that inherently makes an oath seem more significant and searching to most people than does any simple affirmation?

15 What should be regarded as the ultimate motivation for telling the truth? b) What bearing has that ultimate motivation upon what should be one's most fundamental attitude in life?

16 "An eye for an eye, and a tooth for a tooth": considered wholly apart from any standard that Jesus sets over against this law, what judgment, favorable or unfavorable, should one pass upon the law, and for what reasons?

17 If one reacts unfavorably toward this law of retaliation,

how should one formulate what one would propose as a satisfactory substitute for it?

18 Wherein consists the essential difference between one's own formulation of some substitute and that which is here credited to Jesus?

19 "Love," "do good to," "bless," "pray for": among these attitudes, which may be regarded, if any, as beyond the limits of one's personal control?

20 "Even sinners do the same": how define the limits beyond which the disciple of Jesus is expected to go?

21 "Love your enemies": on what base does Jesus ultimately ground his commendation of the extension of love even to one's enemies?

22 "Verily I say unto you, They have received their reward": wherein consists the futility of such reward?

23 "And thy Father, which seeth in secret, shall recompense thee": what exactly is the nature of that recompense which comes to the person whose sole frame of reference in his actions is God?

24 What had happened in the career of Jesus, preceding this discourse, which would naturally result in his speaking about critics and criticism?

25 What were some of the motes concerning which Jesus had been severely criticized by the religious authorities of his day?

26 Judging by the content of this discourse, what were regarded by Jesus as the beams which were blinding those who charged him with being a destroyer?

27 What may be supposed to have been the reason why Jesus used the figure of the eye to convey his thought relative to criticism?

28 "Even so do ye also unto them": according to this saying, where should one go to discover the norms that may reasonably be followed in one's relations with other persons?

29 "Whatsoever ye would that men should do unto you": in the event of this law being accepted as determinative for conduct, what becomes of external moral codes? b) What value then is resident in the ethical standards set forth in this discourse?

30 What areas of the individual life, and consequently of the moral problem, stand outside the bounds of one's conduct in relations with other persons?

31 "Not every one that saith unto me, Lord, Lord": what judgment does Jesus apparently pass here upon the significance of high estimates of his person?

32 What would Jesus substitute for the discovery and statement of significant values as found lodged in him?

33 Over against the annunciation of worth in Jesus, he would himself set the functioning of what element in human personality?

34 What place does Jesus represent belief as holding in the condition he enunciates here for entrance into the kingdom of God?

35 What exactly is the difference between a) endeavoring to live according to the ethical norms of this discourse and b) deciding to live in harmony with the will of God?

36 Which is the more important: a) to decide to do the will of God, or b) to know in advance what is the specific content of the will of God? 2) Which should be prior—knowledge or intention—if one is to stand on safe ground?

37 "The good man out of the good treasure of his heart bringeth forth that which is good; and the evil man out of the evil treasure bringeth forth that which is evil": what is the specification of Jesus, within this discourse, whereby the good man may be produced?

38 What relation do the ethical norms within this discourse bear to the production of the good man?

39 "And doeth them" . . . "and doeth them not": what difference would it make in the thought if one should substitute for these words the phrases "And believeth them" . . . "and believeth them not"?

40 "Founded upon the rock": by the exercise of what function of the personality?

41 "These words of mine": what words of the discourse most completely epitomize the central and determinative thought of the discourse?

42 "That leadeth to destruction" . . . "that leadeth unto life": what do the central terms here mean?

43 "Enter ye in by the narrow gate": where within this discourse may one discover what Jesus meant by the narrow gate?

44 "Few be they that find it": why is that so?

45 "As one having authority": what were the singular qualities in the teaching of Jesus which produced that impression?

CHAPTER VI

CONTEMPORARY OPINIONS ABOUT THE WORTH OF JESUS

§27 *Opinion of a Roman Centurion*

1 "He is worthy": what fundamental qualities of character were possessed by the centurion as evidenced in his attitude and actions as reported to Jesus by the elders of the Jews?

2 "The centurion sent unto him elders of the Jews" . . . "the centurion sent friends to him": what estimate of Jesus by the centurion is indicated through the fact that he thought himself unworthy to come to Jesus directly?

3 "For I am not worthy that thou shouldest come under my roof": for what reason did the centurion desire that Jesus should act at a distance?

4 "A man set under authority": what did the centurion mean by this personal estimate of Jesus?

5 "I have not found so great faith, no, not in Israel": what quality of character in the centurion did Jesus intend to cover here by the term "faith"?

6 Wherein was the faith of the centurion different from the attitude toward Jesus and estimate of him displayed generally by his fellow-countrymen?

7 What reaction should one properly have toward the interpretation that the great faith of the centurion consisted in his belief that Jesus could act at a distance?

§28 *Opinion of John the Baptist*

1 "Art thou he that cometh?": how put that question in a form that will make its meaning unmistakably clear in terms of contemporary thinking in the time of Jesus?

2 What evidence has previously appeared that John had ever sought to identify Jesus with the Christ?

3 What factors in the developing historical situation had contributed toward confronting John with the question as to the relation of Jesus to the messianic hope of his people?

4 John had asked a question which called for a simple af-

firmative or negative as an adequate answer: how describe the nature and intention of the response made by Jesus?

5 "Blessed is he, whosoever shall find none occasion of stumbling in me": how formulate an extended paraphrase of these words that will bring out clearly the intended thought of Jesus?

6 What deduction as to his relation to the messiahship did Jesus intend should be inferred from the content of the response he made to John?

7 What is the relation between the meaning of the answer of Jesus to John on this occasion and his consistent attitude on those previous occasions when men had declared that he was the Christ?

8 "Among them that are born of women there is none greater than John": what are the evidences that Jesus had been himself profoundly affected by the ministry of John?

9 "He that is but little in the kingdom of God is greater than John": what is it that constitutes the difference?

10 "All the prophets and the law prophesied until John": and after that, exactly what?

11 "Wisdom is justified of all her children": how paraphrase the meaning of that saying in the light of its context?

§29 *Opinion of a Sinner* vs *Opinion of a Pharisee*

1 "For she loved much": because of forgiveness? or cause of her forgiveness?

2 "And Jesus said unto the woman, Thy sins are forgiven": what adequate grounds had Jesus for such a significant declaration?

3 "Who is this that even forgiveth sins?": wherein did the conception of Jesus relative to sin and its forgiveness differ fundamentally from that of his contemporary religious teachers?

4 "Thy faith hath saved thee": wherein did the faith of the woman consist? b) What quality or attitude in the woman was that to which Jesus made reference by his use of the term faith?

§30 *On a Tour in Galilee*

On the occasion of this tour in Galilee, Jesus devoted himself to what form of activity?

§31 *Opinion of the Friends of Jesus*

1 "He is beside himself": by which the friends of Jesus expressed themselves as thinking what about Jesus?

2 What were some of the grounds on which the friends of Jesus could base this conclusion of theirs about him?

§32 *Opinion of the Religious Leaders*

1 "By the prince of the devils casteth he out the devils": that was what the scribes from Jerusalem asserted: what other explanation can better be offered to account for the effectiveness of Jesus in dealing with these mental cases?

2 "How can Satan cast out Satan?": what is the only reasonable answer to that devastating question?

3 "By whom do your sons cast them out?": what may one suppose Jesus to have thought would be an adequate explanation of that ability on the part of some of his contemporaries?

4 "Whosoever shall blaspheme against the Spirit of God, it shall not be forgiven him": what exactly was the ultimate nature of that offence of the scribes from Jerusalem which Jesus asserted was blasphemy against the Spirit of God? b) For what inherent reason is that offence, by virtue of its nature, beyond the bounds of other wrongdoing?

CHAPTER VII

THE MYSTERY OF THE KINGDOM OF GOD

§33 *Basis of Real Relationship to Jesus*

1 "Who is my mother and my brethren?": what is the most impressive fact that one may learn about the personal religious life of Jesus from the turn he gave to this situation by formulating and answering this arresting question?

2 How state the conception of God that comes to implicit expression through what Jesus says in Section 33?

3 What must one believe in order to be able to fulfil the conditions here set down for kinship to Jesus?

4 Where and how may one discover what is the content of the will of God?

5 In what measure is knowledge of the will of God dependent upon determination or decision, in advance of knowledge, to do the will of God?

6 What justification is there for differentiating the will of God, as an object of loyalty, from any specific action or any specific body of norms for conduct?

7 What attitude of the personal will does loyalty to the will of God most properly involve: a) iron determination to live in accordance with ideals? or, b) dethronement of the personal will and effortless conformity?

§34 *Discourse on the Kingdom of God*

1 "How shall we liken the kingdom of God? or in what parable shall we set it forth?": in view of these questions, by which Jesus prefaced the discourse, what is the probability as to the intended content of the parables, that is, should one expect to find a) conceptions of the nature of the kingdom already held by the contemporaries of Jesus, or b) distinctive views of the kingdom originated by Jesus and set over against prevailing conceptions?

2 "Whereunto shall I liken the kingdom of God?": do these words suggest that the intended answer of Jesus, conveyed by the parables, was a) the kingdom of God is exactly

what your teachers have always taught you about it, or b) the kingdom of God is essentially something different in nature and in form of realization from contemporary teaching about it?

3 What objection may be offered to the acceptance and application of the norm that one should find, in every parable, some truth about the kingdom of God that is contrary to or corrective of some contemporary view about the kingdom?

4 "Every scribe who hath been made a disciple to the kingdom of God . . . bringeth forth out of his treasure things new and old": what bearing does this saying, with which Jesus concludes the discourse on the kingdom of God, have upon the fundamental question whether Jesus was departing in this discourse from contemporary conceptions of the kingdom?

5 "And Jesus asked them, Have ye understood all these things?": what difficulty in understanding would there have been if the intended thought of Jesus about the kingdom of God was already common knowledge as the possession of his contemporaries?

6 "Explain unto us the parable of the tares of the field": why the call for explanation if the parables are simple stories fashioned to make contemporary truth more vivid?

7 "Who hath ears to hear, let him hear": what does this repeated refrain of the discourse indicate as to the obviousness or otherwise of the thought about the kingdom of God set forth through the parables used by Jesus?

8 "Jesus taught them many things in parables . . . With many parables spake Jesus the word unto them . . . without a parable spake he not unto them": why this adoption exclusively of the parabolic method, on this sole occasion in the reported teaching of Jesus, when dealing with a theme (the kingdom of God) on which the religious leaders of the day already held definite opinions?

9 "Take heed therefore how ye hear": whether is this injunction intended for a) truth expressed in a form that makes its meaning obvious, or b) truth cast in such fashion that its meaning is intended to elude the hearer where preconceptions and prejudices occupy and possess the mind?

10 "All things are done in parables that hearing they may hear and not understand": on the basis of this statement,

credited to Jesus, why did Jesus employ the parabolic form rather than direct and plain statement, in expounding, to those that were without, his own conceptions of the kingdom of God?

11 What danger was there to Jesus personally, from the religious leaders of his day, if he should express his conceptions of the kingdom of God in terms so clear and direct that there could be no doubt for anybody as to his intended meaning?

12 "If any man hath ears to hear, let him hear": who is intended to be excluded from the understanding of the parables on the kingdom of God according to this saying?

13 "Whosoever hath, to him shall be given; and whosoever hath not, from him shall be taken away even that which he thinketh he hath": how formulate an adequate paraphrase of this saying regarded as an integral part of this distinctive discourse?

14 "There is nothing hid, save that it should be manifested; neither was anything made secret, but that it should come to light": in view of this enunciated position of Jesus, what was the ultimate object he had in mind through his resort on this occasion to the hidden and secret method of conveying the truth about the kingdom of God?

15 "Be not afraid of them which kill the body": this threat to life because of the speaking of unwelcome truth about the kingdom of God was averted, for the time being, by Jesus through his employment of what mode of presenting his thought?

16 In the effort to understand any parable, whether should the endeavor be directed a) to discovering the parallels for many features of the parable, or b) to the determination of what is the central and single intention of the parable?

17 In the elucidation of the parables on the kingdom of God, what single criterion for the rejection of any proposed interpretation may most properly be employed?

18 Remembering that any parable about the kingdom of God is likely to contain both things old (contemporary concepts) and things new (the distinctive thought of Jesus), how formulate what is the old and what is the new in the parable of the mustard seed?

19 "Like unto leaven which a woman took and hid": as

against what contemporary conception as to the mode of the realization of the kingdom of God?

20 In the parable of the wheat and tares, the difference of position, as between the householder and the servants, was concerned with what particular point? b) How state the position that the householder rejected?

21 John the Baptist had preached that the kingdom of God would be constituted through what mode of action by the Messiah? b) From the parable of the wheat and tares one should conclude that Jesus held what opinion about the conception of John relative to the mode and time of the realization of the kingdom of God?

22 "He that is but little in the kingdom of God is greater than John": judging from the parable of the wheat and the tares, apparently at least greater in what one fundamental regard?

23 "First the blade, then the ear, then the full corn in the ear": against what contemporary opinion about the nature of the kingdom of God is the parable of the developing grain directed by Jesus?

24 In the parables of the treasure and of the pearl, what is the thing old (contemporary opinion) and what is the thing new (distinctive contribution of Jesus) about the kingdom of God?

25 "Selleth all that he hath" . . . "sold all that he had": whether is this indicative a) of the worth of the kingdom, or b) of the cost of the kingdom?

26 "All that he hath": at what point in the outposts of personality may it be confidently affirmed that any individual has given all to anything or anybody?

CHAPTER VIII

ACTIVITY ON TOURS OF JESUS AND DISCIPLES

§35 *Fear* versus *Faith*

1 "Have ye not yet faith?": faith in whom? or faith in what?

2 "Have ye not yet faith?": what was the evidence that they were lacking in faith?

3 What content must be given to the term faith as used under the circumstances here described?

4 How does the possession of the quality meant here by faith contribute toward the correction of fear?

§36 *Jesus Teaches at Nazareth*

1 "Whence hath this man these things?": what should be regarded as the most adequate answer to that important question?

2 "Is not this the carpenter?": their theory was that religious insight and conviction when manifest were the products of what? b) Of what actually are religious penetration and originality the resultants?

3 "A prophet is not without honour, save in his own country, and among his own kin, and in his own house": how account for that general fact?

§37 *Jesus Teaches Throughout Galilee*

When Jesus made an extensive tour throughout Galilee, what did he regard as the form of activity to which exclusively he should devote himself?

§38 *Disciples Tour in Galilee*

1 "The harvest truly is plenteous, but the labourers are few": whether is that less true or more true in the present generation than in the time of Jesus?

2 "The labourer is worthy of his food": what can be urged against adopting the methods credited here to Jesus as standard

practice in the promotion of religion in all ages and everywhere?

3 "Search out who in it is worthy": in what sense worthy?

4 "Go not from house to house": why this particular injunction?

5 "He that receiveth you receiveth me, and he that receiveth me receiveth him that sent me": for that to be true of the disciples, what relation must their own religious life bear to the personal religion of Jesus? b) What element in the personal religion of Jesus gives the basis for asserting that whoever receives Jesus receives him that sent him?

§39 *Fate of John the Baptist*

"John said unto Herod, It is not lawful for thee to have thy brother's wife: Herod sent and beheaded John in the prison": what then should one say concerning the following estimate of John by Jesus—"What went ye out into the wilderness to behold? a reed shaken with the wind? What went ye out to see? a man clothed in soft raiment? Behold, they which are gorgeously apparelled, and live delicately, are in kings' courts"?

§40 *Report of Associates on Their Tour*

1 "Whatsoever they had taught": what may be supposed to have been the content of the message the disciples delivered to their hearers during their tour?

2 "Come ye yourselves apart into a desert place, and rest a while": what would be the major possible contributions of such procedure?

§41 *Jesus Teaching in the Desert*

1 "Jesus had compassion on them": into what form of activity on his part did this compassion lead Jesus, according to the account?

2 "He departed into the mountain to pray": what were some of the major problems with which Jesus was confronted at this period?

CHAPTER IX

DEMAND BY PHARISEES FOR CONFORMITY AND CREDENTIALS

§42 *Concerning Traditions about Defilement*

1 "The tradition of the elders" . . . "the tradition of the elders" . . . "the precepts of men" . . . "the tradition of men" . . . "your tradition" . . . "your tradition": by what phrases does Jesus set something over against these phrases?

2 "The commandment of God" . . . "the commandment of God" . . . "the word of God": a) was elucidated through, or b) was suffering from, the accumulation of tradition?

3 In the justification offered by Jesus for the action of his disciples in their ignoring of the customs relative to ceremonial cleansings, what is the initial reason put forward on their behalf?

4 "To eat with unwashen hands defileth not the man": in view of the contemporary Jewish position on this matter, what would be the natural outcome of such a drastic and unqualified pronouncement by Jesus?

5 "It cannot defile him, because it goeth not into his heart": for the second half of this saying, what would one substitute if seeking to put the thought in modern psychological terminology?

6 "Evil things proceed from within, out of the heart of men, and defile": if one should feel compelled, because of its vagueness, to abandon the use of the figurative term "heart" as the generative center of personality, what might properly be used in its place to cover adequately the intended thought of Jesus in this saying?

7 If nothing going into the man can defile him, what justification is there for believing that anything taken into the man can religiously benefit him?

8 "Every plant which my Father planted not, shall be rooted up": for the mind of Jesus, this implies the ultimate triumph of what?

§43 *Withdrawal toward Tyre and Sidon*

"And he could not be hid": what may be supposed to have been the object of Jesus in withdrawing to the north at this time?

§44 *Return Journey through Decapolis*

Why the movement of Jesus through the midst of the borders of Decapolis?

§45 *Pharisees Demand Signs from Jesus*

1 "Seeking of him a sign from heaven": what may be supposed to have been the nature of that which the critics of Jesus sought on this occasion?

2 "An evil and adulterous generation seeketh after a sign": what is there essentially wrong in seeking for some sign from one who assumes religious leadership?

3 "There shall no sign be given unto this generation": what are some of the signs that are usually supposed to have been given to that generation by Jesus?

§46 *The Leaven of the Pharisees*

1 "We have no bread": this response of the disciples to the injunction of Jesus relative to the leaven of the Pharisees indicates what inference on the part of the disciples?

2 "Do ye not yet perceive, neither understand? Having eyes, see ye not? and having ears, hear ye not?": of what important discourse by Jesus, already fully studied, are these terms rather vividly a reminder? b) What was the sole theme of that discourse? c) In what teaching form was that discourse cast?

3 "How is it that ye do not perceive that I spake not to you concerning bread": since the meaning of Jesus had no reference to the leaven of bread but rather to the leaven of the teaching of the Pharisees, and since this warning follows upon the demand from the Pharisees for some sign, what central conception held by the Pharisees was Jesus apparently condemning through his injunction to the disciples?

CHAPTER X

FORECASTS OF CONFLICT WITH THE JERUSALEM AUTHORITIES

§47 *Opinion of Disciples about Jesus*

1 "Who do men say that I am?": what may be supposed to have been the purpose of Jesus in putting this question to his disciples?

2 "And others, Elijah": in which event Jesus would bear what relation to the expected Messiah?

3 "But others, One of the prophets": what judgment may one most properly pass upon this estimate of Jesus?

4 "But who say ye that I am?": what opinion about Jesus may be regarded as that which had originally led the disciples to consider Jesus favorably?

5 "Thou art the Christ": for how long, and for what reasons, had the disciples cherished this singular conviction about Jesus?

6 "Then charged Jesus the disciples that they should tell no man that he was the Christ": what was the ground objection of Jesus to the declaration by the disciples to others that he was the Christ?

7 On what previous occasions had Jesus taken the same attitude toward assertions by others that he was the Christ as is here credited to him? b) What is the meaning of that repeated and consistent attitude?

§48 *Jesus Forecasts Events at Jerusalem*

1 The fate which Jesus foresaw as awaiting him in Jerusalem and which he is here reported as sketching was a deduction by him from what known facts?

2 "Master: this shall never be unto thee": does this outburst indicate that Jesus had been depicting a succession of events having their climax in a) something tragic and deplorable, or b) something stupendous and splendid?

3 "Thou mindest the things of men": what were the things

of men that Jesus had in mind when he administered this stinging rebuke?

4 "Thou mindest not the things of God": enumerate those attitudes, actions, and events which were regarded by Jesus as the things of God.

5 "Get thee behind me, Satan": in the light of this estimate of Peter by Jesus, what degree of significance is it likely that Jesus attached to the declaration of Peter (Section 47) that Jesus was the Christ?

6 "From that time began Jesus": from what time? b) Jesus began to do what, stated broadly? c) What then was the object of Jesus in raising the question (Section 47) as to how he was being regarded?

§49 *Some Costs of Discipleship*

1 "Let him deny himself": deny himself what?

2 What is the difference between denying one's self something and denying one's self?

3 If one sets out to deny one's self rather than to deny something to one's self, what is the underlying assumption as to one's essential nature?

4 As a result of the process of denying one's self, is it to be assumed that the actor is gainer? or loser? b) If one says loser, what is the motive for the action? c) If one says gainer, how can gain come through denial or negation?

5 "Whosoever would save his life shall lose it; but whosoever shall lose his life shall save it": does Jesus by this saying a) negative the ambition to possess fulness of life, or b) define the wrong and the right processes for the achievement of that end?

6 "Whosoever shall lose his life shall save it": what is the motive here? b) What is the process here? c) What is the outcome here? d) Is the motive here selfish or unselfish? e) Is the process here selfish or unselfish? f) Is the outcome here selfish or unselfish?

7 "Whosoever shall lose his life shall save it": if the motive and outcome here are not condemnable, what is it that may lead to the frustration of the end?

8 "Whosoever would save his life shall lose it": what is the outcome here? b) What is the process here? c) That which is process here becomes what in the second half of the saying?

d) Frustration of the end therefore results from confusing what with what?

9 Since to think of process (first half of saying) and of outcome (second half of saying) in the same terms (save the life) exhibits a confusion in the mind between means and end, what other means toward the desired end is set forth by Jesus in the second half of the saying?

10 "Whosoever shall lose his life shall save it": so that the single highly important point to determine is an adequate content for the phrase "lose his life": what does that phrase mean?

11 "Lose his life": does that mean lose the physical life for a person or a cause? Or does it mean lose one's self in the service of others? Or does it mean become utterly possessed by the pursuit of some calling or some ambition or aim? Or does it mean enter into some profound mystical experience? Or does it mean something other than and more fundamental than any of these attitudes, acts, or states?

12 "Whosoever would save his life" (wrong method) as over against "Whosoever shall lose his life" (sound method): perhaps some contribution toward the understanding of the sound method may be had by endeavoring to give definite content to the wrong method: precisely what does "save his life" mean in the first half of the saying?

13 "What is a man profited, if he gain the whole world, and lose or forfeit his own self?": what does the usual practice of men indicate as the customary response to that question?

14 "The whole world" . . . "his own self": what do these contrasted terms suggest as to the conception of personality held by Jesus?

15 "Lose or forfeit his own self": does this suggest a) selfhood as something complete by virtue of its own nature, or b) selfhood as something to be achieved by some method?

§50 *The Problem of Tribute Payment*

1 Judging by this report, what had been the general attitude of Jesus toward the customary mode of securing the necessary funds for the upkeep of the temple services in Jerusalem?

2 "Jesus said unto him, Therefore the sons are free": by his use of what he evidently intended as in some measure an

analogy, Jesus conveyed what thought as to statutory methods of assuring the support of religion?

3 "Therefore the sons are free": the sons are free, relative to the advancement of religion, to act after what manner?

4 "Therefore the sons are free": the genesis of donation, in the area of religion, should be found in what inner sense of the giver?

§51 *Teaching on Greatness*

1 "Salt is good . . . Have salt in yourselves": on what occasion previously had Jesus used the figure of salt relative to the disciples?

2 "If any man would be first, he shall be last of all, and minister of all": how state this saying in language altogether different but bearing the same meaning as Jesus intended?

3 Is the attitude of Jesus here toward the natural and deep-seated desire and ambition of man for place and power a) one of condemnation of the impulse, or b) one of direction for its richest achievement?

4 What degree of relationship is there between the statement here of the way of Jesus to the achievement of greatness and the statements elsewhere of the way of Jesus to the achievement of selfhood or life?

§52 *Teaching on Tolerance*

1 "We saw one casting out devils": indicative of what general fact relative to the practice of exorcism in the days of Jesus?

2 "In thy name": what had led to the potency in mental cases of this particular formula at the hands of others?

3 "Because he followed not with us": this is the watchword of what attitude in the area of theology and religion?

4 "He that is not against us is for us": what bearing does this saying have upon the attitude of those in religious activity who tend to be critical of others whose mode of religious functioning is essentially different from their own?

§53 *Teaching on Forgiveness*

1 "Until seventy times seven": who is benefited the more by the attitude and action here commended by Jesus— a) the forgiven person, or b) the forgiving person?

2 Wherein consists the essentially destructive nature of unforgiveness?

3 What are the possible outcomes of the attitude of forgiveness, while the offender is still unrepentant, a) upon the one sinned against, and b) upon the offender?

§54 *Parable on Forgiveness*

1 What may one legitimately learn from this parable about the thought of Jesus concerning the attitude of God toward the person who does wrong?

2 Upon what foundation does Jesus here base his teaching as to the proper attitude and spirit of one man who has been wronged toward another man who has wronged him?

CHAPTER XI

DEPARTURE FROM GALILEE FOR JERUSALEM

§55 *General Statement of Journey*

1 "As he was wont, he taught them": from which it may be deduced that Jesus considered what activity as the primary mode of his functioning in life?

2 "Stedfastly set his face": why the use of these terms in the description of a journey to Jerusalem?

§56 *Teaching on Tolerance*

1 "As though he were going to Jerusalem": why did that intention create an unfavorable attitude on the part of the Samaritans?

2 "Wilt thou that we bid fire to come down from heaven, and consume them?": in what era has that attitude been absent from major elements in the Christian world community?

3 "What manner of spirit": from where or from whom should one learn the manner of spirit befitting a disciple of Jesus?

4 Intolerance is ultimately grounded in what subversive element of human nature?

5 As against ostracism, or persecution, or overt acts toward those who oppose, what is the constructive method of dealing with opposition?

§57 *Some Tests of Discipleship*

1 "Have not where to lay my head": discipleship to Jesus holds within it what forms of guarantee of worldly goods?

2 "Leave the dead to bury their own dead": if one were to come upon this as an isolated saying of Jesus, disassociated from any assumed historical context, what meaning would one be justified in assigning to it?

3 "No man, having put his hand to the plough, and looking back, is fit for the kingdom of God": since this saying bears no exclusive relationship to the occasion to which it is here at-

tached, its intention may be derived otherwise: how restate the thought in terms not figurative?

4 What is that distinctive quality about the condition for entrance into the kingdom of God which makes it true that "looking back" is an evidence of the non-fulfillment of the condition?

§58 *The Way of Eternal Life*

1 "What is written in the law?": one of the laws chosen by the lawyer is from one book and the other from a different book: one has to do with what relationship and the other with what different relationship? b) The selection and conjunction of the two separated sayings is to be credited to whom?

2 "With all thy heart, and with all thy soul, and with all thy strength, and with all thy mind": by these several successive terms—heart . . . soul . . . strength . . . mind—each conceived in its totality ("all"), one covers how much of the human personality?

3 "Thy neighbour as thyself": according to this saying, the ethical norms for the determination of one's treatment of other people are to be discovered by looking where for them?

4 "Thou shalt love God . . . Thou shalt love thy neighbour": since in these sayings the word "love" covers something which it is assumed can be commanded and controlled, what sense of that word is thereby excluded from consideration as the intended meaning?

5 If one were to come upon the answer of the lawyer, for the first time, in a manuscript where the central term "love" was not legible, what should one venture to supply as the word or phrase (different in each half of the saying) which would most fittingly convey some meaning worthy of the impressive context?

6 "This do, and thou shalt live": since the lawyer had derived his definition of the way of life from the documents of his own religion, and since Jesus had accepted the lawyer's definition as completely adequate, what contribution may here be credited to Jesus bearing upon the way of life?

7 "This do, and thou shalt live": what place is there within the lawyer's definition for assigning any function to Jesus in the process of the attainment of life?

8 "Thou shalt love thy neighbour as thyself": what saying, attributed to Jesus, conveys substantially the same thought?

9 "Thou shalt love the Lord thy God with all thy heart, and with all thy soul, and with all thy strength, and with all thy mind": in what passages may one find the same completeness and absoluteness of attitude set forth in language formulated by Jesus?

§59 *The Definition of Neighbour*

1 "Who is my neighbour?": what are some of the contents that might, with seeming legitimacy, be given to that term?

2 "Who is my neighbour?": judging from the context of the saying concerning the loving of neighbour, as found in Leviticus 19:17-18, the Jewish people in the time of Jesus were accustomed to define neighbour as covering what range of persons?

3 What dangers would there have been for Jesus in the direct and explicit statement that the definition of neighbour in terms of religion and race was not true to the mind of God?

b) How did Jesus convey that conviction with the minimum of offence?

4 What was achieved in the parable by the setting of a Samaritan over against two Jews of religious prominence?

5 What effect does the Samaritan's answer in action to the question "Who is my neighbour?" have upon any definition of neighbour in terms of religion and race?

6 What are the outermost boundaries of the term neighbour for Jesus—drawing one's deduction from the thought current in his time and from the indirection of the parable?

§60 *Many Things* vs *One Thing*

1 "Anxious and troubled about many things: but one thing is needful": what is the one thing that is needful?

2 In order not to make the comment of Jesus trivial and dubious, the contrast of the one with the many can hardly be regarded as concerned with the superficial and the external: while the genesis of the comment is commonplace enough, the turning of the incident to account by Jesus may reach into the profound: wherein consists the essential danger of "many things" in the realm of religion?

§61 *Elements of Prevailing Prayer*

1 "In praying use not vain repetitions": why are vain repetitions open to condemnation?

2 "God your Father knoweth what things ye have need of, before ye ask him": wherein then consists the validity and value of prayer?

3 Forgiveness of the sins of the petitioner by God is made dependent by Jesus upon what attitude on the part of the petitioner? b) Why should this be the law of forgiveness?

4 What may properly be regarded as the central and most significant petition within the prayer that is here credited to Jesus? b) What is the justification for the choice made?

5 What is the difference in content between the petition "Thy kingdom come" and the petition "Thy will be done, as in heaven, so on earth"?

6 "Thy will be done": whether is this petition directed to a) the passive acceptance by a person of events that happen, or b) the determinative norm for a person that fashions the events which are yet to happen?

7 "Ask . . . seek . . . knock": these acts are indicative of what fundamental attitude on the part of the person who does them? b) Over against that attitude as its antithesis there stands what?

8 "How much more shall your Father give good things": who is the ultimate determiner as to what things asked for are good and what are not good?

9 "Believe that ye have received them, and ye shall have them": what is the nature of those things which one does not have until one believes that one has already received them?

§62 *Limitations of Exorcism*

1 Abandoning the concepts of the time of Jesus about mental cases, describe the phenomena and the outcome of treatment, here set forth, in modern medical terms.

2 What bearing do these observations of Jesus have upon the limits he set to his activity other than teaching?

§63 *Basis of Real Relationship to Jesus*

1 In what measure were the womb and the breasts (the mother) determinative in the production of that which the

woman was exalting, namely, the essential and ultimate character of Jesus?

2 What bearing does the attitude of Jesus here have upon the dogma and practice of the worship of Mary the mother of Jesus?

3 "They that hear the word of God": from what source and under what condition and by what means hear the word of God?

4 "And keep it": what is the intended sense of the central word here?

5 Everything else, however significant and worthy of recognition, is regarded by Jesus as secondary to what?

CHAPTER XII

DEEP FEELING AND DIRECT TEACHING

§64 *Effects of the Mission of Jesus*

1 "Think ye that I am come to cast peace on the earth? I tell you, Nay; but rather division": what justification then is there for regarding Jesus as the prince of peace?

2 "A man's foes shall be they of his own household": the divisions take place over what issues and on what grounds?

3 "I came to cast fire upon the earth": what were the most essential elements in the nature of the fire that Jesus cast upon the earth?

4 "I have a baptism to be baptized with": to what was Jesus making reference in this statement? b) And what was his attitude toward it?

§65 *The Signs of the Times*

1 "How is it that ye cannot discern the signs of the times?": what specific area of the national thought and practice did Jesus have in mind when he spoke of the national failure to discern the signs of the times?

2 What degree of justification can be advanced for the supposition that the mind of Jesus was dwelling here upon the national political situation?

§66 *Warnings of National Disaster*

1 "Galilaeans whose blood Pilate had mingled with their sacrifices": for some offence of what general nature would the Roman governor of Judaea act thus drastically toward a group of Galilaeans?

2 "Ye shall all in like manner perish": perish at the hands of whom? b) Perish for what manner of offence?

3 "Except ye repent": repent with reference to what particular positions and what kind of actions?

4 What may be supposed to have been the offence for which the eighteen men had been imprisoned in the tower of Siloam?

5 "They were offenders": offenders against whom and against what?

6 "Ye shall all likewise perish": since all the men that dwelt in Jerusalem could not suffer death by a similar type of accident, the "likewise" must refer to a likeness concerning reason for death rather than manner of death: what factors in the situation were making for the disaster on a national scale that came in a few decades?

§67 *Teaching about Reliance on Wealth*

1 "A man's life consisteth not in the abundance of the things which he possesseth": what is the single most absolute and ultimate thing wherein the life of a man may properly consist?

2 "So is he that layeth up treasure for himself, and is not rich toward God": by what method or process may one become actually rich toward God?

3 "Where thy treasure is, there will thy heart be also": so that the matter of importance for Jesus is that which engages the heart: what is meant here by the heart? b) What may one justifiably substitute for that older designation?

§68 *Saying on Light and Darkness*

1 "The lamp of thy body is thine eye: when thine eye is single, thy whole body also is full of light; but when it is evil, thy body also is full of darkness": if this saying had begun with the words "The lamp of thy mind is thy will", how should one refashion the rest of the saying?

2 "Look whether the light that is in thee be not darkness": in what measure is the light that is within one something that is under one's control? b) What is the seat within personality of its control?

3 "If the light that is in thee be darkness, how great is the darkness!": what is the effective cure for getting out of this deplorable state?

§69 *Limits of the Kingdom of God*

1 "And Jesus went on his way through cities and villages teaching": so that it may be affirmed that the major mode of functioning chosen by Jesus was what mode?

2 "Master, are they few that be saved?": for an interest in the theoretical question about numbers, Jesus by his answer substituted what?

3 "Strive to enter in by the narrow door": what was the narrow door as Jesus conceived it?

4 "Shall not be able": for what reason not able?

5 "From the east and west, and from the north and south": in what measure has this ultimate outlook of Jesus had realization?

§70 *Forecast of his Death by Jesus*

1 "Herod would fain kill thee": what may be supposed to have been the reasons why Herod wished to put Jesus to death?

2 "The third day I am perfected": what may we learn about Jesus from his own interpretation of his impending fate at Jerusalem?

§71 *Teaching in Criticism of Anxiety*

1 "Be not anxious . . . Which of you by being anxious . . . Why are ye anxious? . . . Be not therefore anxious . . . Be not therefore anxious": the condemnation of Jesus here is directed solely against what attitude of the mind? b) What relation does that attitude bear to planning and foresight?

2 In what measure do the lilies of the field have anxiety? b) In what degree do the birds of the heaven have anxiety?

3 "God feedeth the birds of the heaven . . . God doth clothe the grass of the field": in what sense, and in what sense only, may these statements be regarded as true?

4 "All these things shall be added unto you": in what sense, and in what sense only, can that statement be regarded as true?

5 Whether is it a) the state of nature, or b) the state of man, or c) the state of society, which creates the conditions that tend inevitably to drive men into anxiety about food and clothing?

6 "Seek ye first his kingdom, and his righteousness": what effect can that have upon a) nature, or b) society, or c) man, relative to food and clothing?

§72 *Teachings at the Table of a Pharisee*

1 "Every one that exalteth himself shall be humbled": what exactly is it that is fundamentally wrong inwardly with the person who exalts himself?

2 What is the difference between the source of self exaltation and the sound method of self realization?

3 "And a recompense be made thee . . . they have not wherewith to recompense thee": recompense for hospitable treatment should come from what source only and in what form only?

§73 *The Costs of Discipleship*

1 "First sit down and count the cost . . . sit down first and take counsel": this element in the advice of Jesus makes against decisions relative to the religious life reached under what circumstances?

2 How can one count the cost when one has really never been adequately informed as to the nature and extent of the cost, or has been wrongly informed? b) What then is the first essential for following the advice of Jesus about decision?

3 "If any man cometh unto me, and hateth not his own father, and mother, and wife, and children, and brethren, and sisters, yea, and his own life also, he cannot be my disciple": a) in what sense is the word hateth used in this saying? b) What was the purpose of Jesus in making so extensive an enumeration of those whom and that which must be hated? c) To whom and to what must the primary loyalty be completely given—to Jesus, or to a cause, or to God, or to whom or what?

4 "So therefore whosoever he be of you that renounceth not all that he hath, he cannot be my disciple": on what previous occasion, and in definition of what, is Jesus reported to have used the central term employed here—all that he hath?

5 "That renounceth not all that he hath": precisely what content does the term renounceth hold when used in this connection?

6 "All that he hath": what is the outermost periphery of renunciation beyond which it is not possible for any person to go?

7 "He that hath ears to hear, let him hear": wherein consists the appropriateness of that saying as the conclusion of this talk?

CHAPTER XIII

MANY TRUTHS TAUGHT IN PARABLES

§74 *Parables on the Worth of Sinners*

1 "This man receiveth sinners, and eateth with them": on what previous occasions had Jesus been reprimanded by the same groups for his attitude toward these outcast classes? b) In what form did Jesus then cast his defence?

2 "Now all the publicans and sinners were drawing near unto Jesus for to hear him": what does this fact indicate as to a) the personal character and b) the religious thought of Jesus?

3 The attitude of the religious authorities contemporary with Jesus set the publicans and sinners as altogether beyond the religious pale: judging from the parables of the lost sheep and the lost coin, what is regarded by Jesus as the place where the bounds of religious demarcation should be drawn?

4 In the parable of the lost son, the younger son asserted, "Father, I have sinned against heaven, and in thy sight": the elder son asserted, "Thy son hath devoured thy living with harlots": the father by his attitude asserted what relative to those facts?

5 How state the primary and outstanding truth which it may be supposed that Jesus is endeavouring to convey indirectly through the parable of the lost son?

§75 *God* versus *Mammon*

1 "No servant can serve two masters . . . Ye cannot serve God and mammon": why should one have any master whatever? b) Why should one serve anybody or anything? c) Why not live utterly masterless?

2 What are some of the possible masters of human life, other than God or mammon?

3 "Ye cannot serve God and mammon": but one can serve God and what?

4 "That which is exalted among men is an abomination in

the sight of God": true of much, or true of most, or true of everything?

§76 *Parable on the Futility of Duty*

1 "Doth he thank the servant because he did the things that were commanded?": what is customary in this regard in the relation between servant and master? b) What less or what more would be commendatory?

2 "When ye shall have done all the things that are commanded you": for the Jewish people in the time of Jesus, the commandments that governed all phases of their life were located in what writings? b) These writings had their sanction in what belief as to their origin?

3 "We are unprofitable servants; we have done that which it was our duty to do": what more should the Jewish people have done than keep the commandments and statutes embodied in their religious law?

4 Wherein consists that futility in duty which constrains one to regard it as altogether unprofitable?

5 What is the highway which leads to that which stands outside the bounds of duty and within the realm of nonprescribed freedom?

§77 *Several Sayings of Jesus*

1 "The law and the prophets were until John": what was supposed to be the status of the law and the prophets, subsequent to John, according to the implications of this saying?

2 The actual status of the law, subsequent to John, seems to be indicated by the second half of the saying—"It is easier for heaven and earth to pass away, than for one tittle of the law to fall": what recorded experiences of Jesus with the tenacity of the religious authorities when he had ventured on what seemed like challenges to the validity of the law may have formed the genesis of this saying?

3 "Wherefore it is lawful to do good on the sabbath day": despite the fact that the sabbath law did expressly forbid all work on the sabbath: Jesus elsewhere formulated his ultimate norm for the sabbath in what terms?

4 "He that is not with me is against me": what is there about the essential nature of the personal religion of Jesus which

excludes the possibility of any person really standing in any neutral zone?

5 "Which come to you in sheep's clothing": what is the most common form of sheep's clothing in the area of the religion that bears the name of Jesus?

§78 *Parable on Deferred Judgement*

On what contemporary situation may it be supposed that the mind of Jesus was resting when he fashioned this parable?

§79 *Time of the Kingdom of God*

1 "The kingdom of God is in the midst of you": what must have been the content for Jesus of the phrase "the kingdom of God" in order for it to be possible for him to speak of it as being "in the midst of you"?

2 "The kingdom of God cometh not with observation": how did John the Baptist think and announce the kingdom of God would come? b) What other contemporary expectations about the kingdom of God involved its coming in spectacular forms that would be observed?

3 "The kingdom of God cometh not with observation" . . . "The kingdom of God is in the midst of you" . . . "They shall see the kingdom of God come with power": interpreted in the light of the first and second of these sayings, what is the most probable meaning of the phrase "come with power" in the third of them?

§80 *Parables on Importunity in Prayer*

1 "They ought always to pray, and not to faint" . . . "Because of his importunity he will": why should it be true that persistence and importunity in prayer avail something not to be otherwise had?

2 How bring into harmonious relationship the ideal of steady importunity and the saying elsewhere attributed to Jesus,—"God your Father knoweth what things ye have need of, before ye ask him"?

§81 *Several Sayings of Jesus*

1 "All things are possible to him that believeth": since this statement, if taken literally, is obviously not in accordance with

the facts of experience or of observation, what was the purpose of Jesus in casting his thought in such absolute form?

2 Why should a religious person be likened to a city set on a hill?

3 "With what measure ye meet, it shall be measured unto you": whether is this reciprocal process between man's gifts to man and God's bestowal upon man a) inherent and automatic, or b) personal and arbitrary?

4 "One of these my brethren, even these least": with what content, that is, with what boundaries, is the term "brethren" used in this saying?

§82 *Parable on the Basis of Justification*

1 "God, I thank thee, that I am not as the rest of men": instead of taking the rest of men as the norm by which to determine one's status, with what norm ought one to confront one's self?

2 When one tests one's self by the determinative norm set elsewhere by Jesus, what self-estimate is inevitable and ever recurrent?

3 Of what fundamental error in religious thought is the listing of virtues, whether achieved or unachieved, a deadly symptom?

CHAPTER XIV

TEACHING AND JOURNEYING ON TO JERUSALEM

§83 *Teachings about Divorce*

1 "For your hardness of heart he wrote you this commandment": when any religious leader or group undertakes to regulate the life of a community by some code of specific commandments, what happens a) to the higher ranges of ethical sensitivity and insight, and b) to the concept of what constitutes essential religion?

2 "What therefore God hath joined together": joined together by a ceremony instituted by man? or joined together, subsequent to a ceremony, by an act in the creation of which man had no part?

3 "Let not man put asunder": how can man attempt to put asunder, in any real sense, that which he has had no real part in joining together?

4 "And marry another" . . . "and marry another": why should the condemnation fall not upon the separation but upon the second marriage? b) And why should it be regarded as an adulterous act?

5 In his statements about divorce, was Jesus a) proposing statutory enactments for a community, or b) enunciating his ideals for individual conduct?

§84 *Essential for Entrance into Kingdom*

What definitely is that quality in character which Jesus apparently wishes to commend as essential for entrance into the kingdom of God?

§85 *Relation of Possessions to Eternal Life*

1 "Why callest thou me good? none is good save one, even God": how formulate the revelation of the character of Jesus that is made by this statement?

2 "One thing thou lackest: go, sell whatsoever thou hast, and give to the poor": if the rich man had announced his intention of doing at once, and with literalness, exactly and all that

Jesus had suggested, what may one suppose would have been the words that Jesus would have then addressed to the man?

3 What are some of the forms of response that might legitimately have been made against the proposal of Jesus taken literally?

4 "One thing thou lackest": in view of the nature of the rich man's actual response, what was really the one thing that he lacked?

5 "Children, how hard is it to enter into the kingdom of God!": what is the reason that such is the case?

§86 *Parable on the Basis of Reward*

1 What commendable quality or attitude did all of the labourers have in common when they stood in the marketplace before any of them had been assigned to work?

2 Against what contemporary religious theory about the basis of reward was this parable directed by Jesus?

3 How state the position of Jesus, as set forth in this parable, relative to what constitutes the ground of religious acceptability with God?

§87 *Teaching on Standards of Greatness*

1 "Grant unto us that we may sit, one on thy right hand, and one on thy left hand, in thy kingdom": what does this request indicate as to the expectation of the disciples relative to what was to be achieved by Jesus when he reached Jerusalem?

2 "Are ye able to drink the cup that I drink? or to be baptized with the baptism that I am baptized with?": what was the cup? b) What was the baptism? c) So that Jesus was asking the disciples whether they were ready for what?

3 "Whosoever would become great among you, shall be your minister: and whosoever would be first among you, shall be servant of all": of two possible procedures relative to observed ambition in men, which does Jesus follow: a) to condemn the impulse toward place and power, or b) to give direction as to the mode of its expression and achievement?

4 "I am in the midst of you as he that serveth": with Jesus personally, was service a) the mode by which he sought to achieve life, or b) the normal expression of life already achieved?

5 What is the difference between the method of attaining

life and the method of attaining greatness, in the thought of Jesus?

§88 *The Rich Publican of Jericho*

1 "He is gone in to lodge with a man that is a sinner": on what previous occasions had Jesus been criticized for this same form of action? b) How had he justified himself on each of those occasions?

2 With what argument does Jesus meet the criticism on this occasion at Jericho?

3 "Salvation is come to this house": how state, in another form, what is meant by these words?

§89 *Time of the Kingdom of God*

1 "They supposed that the kingdom of God was immediately to appear": that expectation was the basis of what request that had recently been made to Jesus?

2 "They supposed that the kingdom of God was immediately to appear": that supposition indicates that the disciples of Jesus held what view as to the nature of the kingdom of God?

3 In the teaching of Jesus explicitly about the kingdom of God, he had sought to convey what conception of a) the nature, and b) the mode of realization, of that kingdom?

4 What understanding of the parable attributed to Jesus brings it into the definite service of the historical situation to which it is here attached?

5 "And when Jesus had thus spoken, he went on before, going up to Jerusalem": with what expectation on his part as to the outcome of his activity in Jerusalem?

CHAPTER XV

CHALLENGE OF THE JERUSALEM LEADERS BY JESUS

§90 *Jesus Enters Jerusalem as Popular Leader*

1 "Blessed is he that cometh in the name of the Lord": by which outburst on the part of the multitude they gave expression to what specific estimate of Jesus? b) What relation, if any, does that estimate bear to contemporary conceptions of the nature and work of the Christ?

2 "Teacher, rebuke thy disciples": for saying exactly what about Jesus?

3 "The stones will cry out": and their message relative to Jesus will have precisely what content?

4 "Till ye shall say, Blessed is he that cometh in the name of the Lord": and mean by that saying, what estimate of Jesus?

5 "The things which belong unto peace": peace with whom? b) What was the most fundamental ground of the enmity?

6 "They shall not leave in thee one stone upon another": Jesus foresaw the destruction of the temple and of Jerusalem as the outcome of an attitude of his people toward Roman rule that had its basis and its fervor in what conception of the kingdom of God?

7 "Because thou knewest not the time of thy visitation": from that visitation they might have learned what about the essential nature of the kingdom of God and the mode of its realization?

8 "This is the prophet, Jesus, from Nazareth of Galilee": what is the relation in meaning of this estimate of Jesus, voiced by the multitudes, to that which found expression in the acclamation "Blessed is he that cometh in the name of the Lord," used as the multitude approached Jerusalem?

§91 *Jesus Casts Commerce from the Temple*

1 What motives did the temple authorities have for allowing commerce to encroach upon the temple area?

2 What did Jesus hope to accomplish by his actions and his words on this occasion?

3 What actually was the result for Jesus of such drastic action?

§92 *Jesus Teaches in the Temple*

1 During the final week of his life, Jesus apparently regarded what as the most potent form of his personal functioning?

2 "For they feared him": what did the chief priests and the scribes and the principal men of the people fear would result if they did not take measures to destroy Jesus?

§93 *Jewish Rulers Challenge Authority of Jesus*

1 "By what authority doest thou these things?": when any religion has reached the stage that its primary appeal is to authority in some form, what is probable as to its possession of self-evidencing vitality?

2 "By what authority doest thou these things?": what justification may be advanced for the attitude of Jesus in refusing to give any answer whatsoever to that question?

3 "By what authority doest thou these things?": if Jesus had consented to formulate some answer to that question, what may one surmise would have been the content of that reply?

§94 *Parables in Condemnation of Jewish Leaders*

1 "Whether of the twain did the will of his father?": this test was set over against what on the part of each of the two sons? So that what in religion counts more than what?

2 "Whether of the twain did the will of his father?": the son ultimately given to action rather than to profession finds the only adequate norm for his action as located where? b) What is the implication of the parable, on that point, in the field of religion?

3 Of what historical facts, situations, and prospects may the story of the vineyard be regarded as a sketch in parabolic form?

4 What is that interpretation of events which is bodied forth through the parable of the marriage feast?

5 "They took Jesus for a prophet": what has history had to say about that judgment in the centuries since that day?

§95 *Efforts to Accumulate Evidence Against Jesus*

1 "So as to deliver him up to the rule and to the authority of the governor": what was the purpose of the Jewish leaders in their effort to get Jesus into the hands of the Roman governor?

2 "Is it lawful for us to give tribute unto Caesar?": what did the Roman law require? b) In view of the fact that there could be no doubt whatever about the Roman law, why should the question be raised about the legality of tribute payment?

3 According to the Jewish religious conception of the state, who actually was regarded as the real and only head of the state? b) Payment of tribute would be interpreted as recognition of whom as the head? c) So that the issue ultimately, for the Jewish mind, was a) political? or b) religious? Which?

4 Had Jesus advised refusal to pay tribute to Rome, he would have been regarded, and hence treated, as a political revolutionary subject to arrest at the hands of the governor. Had Jesus given counsel to pay the tribute, he would be open to the charge of disloyalty to the conception of God as the head of the state and the Jewish people as the prospective kingdom of God. How did Jesus deal with this dilemma?

5 "Render unto Caesar the things that are Caesar's; and unto God the things that are God's": is this response of Jesus a) an evasion or a compromise to avoid the creation of a critical situation, or b) the expression of some fundamental conviction about the essential nature of the kingdom of God?

6 "Render unto Caesar the things that are Caesar's; and unto God the things that are God's": out of what conception as to the actual nature of the kingdom of God does this response of Jesus naturally flow?

7 In the discussion about life after death, the specific problem as presented by the Sadducees was met by Jesus through what fundamental conception as to the nature of the resurrection life?

8 Passing from the specific to the general, Jesus seeks to establish confidence in life after death as a reality by what content of argument?

9 "God is not the god of the dead, but of the living": considered as a saying in itself, stripped of all context, these words might be understood to mean what that is of significance?

10 "Is it not for this cause that ye err, that ye know not the scriptures, nor the power of God?": what degree of insight on any fundamental religious problem is likely to belong to those who know neither human experience as embodied in history nor that immediate experience which is available through some elemental personal attitude?

11 "He that is without sin among you, let him first cast a stone at her": if it should be hypothetically assumed that any individual were without sin, what may one surmise would be the attitude of that person toward killing another person because they had sinned?

12 "Neither do I condemn thee: go thy way; from henceforth sin no more": condemn thee to what? b) State the judgment of Jesus upon the act of the woman in itself, as implicit in the final phrase of his words to her.

13 "Thou shalt love the Lord thy God . . . Thou shalt love thy neighbour": love thy neighbour, according to what norm? b) Love God, with what measure of the personality?

14 "Thou shalt love": what stands in the way of interpreting the central term here as meaning a feeling, an emotion? b) In what measure can love as emotion be subject to command or control?

15 "Thou shalt love": what term or terms can be substituted for love that will convey its intended meaning, as deduced from the rest of the saying, with greater clarity and precision for the modern mind?

16 What is gained for the conduct of life by an individual through an attitude toward God that is not already achieved through an attitude toward neighbour?

17 "What commandment is the first of all? The first is . . . The second is": why not reverse the order and say, The first is this, Thou shalt love thy neighbour? b) Why argue that it is more important to define adequately relationship to God than to indicate the norm for relationship to neighbour?

18 How strong is the probability that the endeavour to fulfil the second commandment will result in the adoption of the first commandment? b) What degree of likelihood is there that the absolute fulfilment of the first commandment would automatically result in the actual fulfilment of the second of these commandments?

19 "To love God . . . to love neighbour, is much more

than all whole burnt offerings and sacrifices": in the light of the teaching of Jesus, of what other supposedly absolute essentials of religion may the same observation be confidently made?

20 "Thou art not far from the kingdom of God": what specifically was that quality made manifest by the scribe which formed the basis for this striking affirmation by Jesus?

21 "Thou art not far from the kingdom of God": what more was needed?

CHAPTER XVI

DISCOURSE IN CONDEMNATION OF SCRIBES AND PHARISEES

§96 *Discourse in Condemnation of Scribes and Pharisees*

1 "All their works they do for to be seen of men": instead of reward in the form of the good opinion of men and recognition from men, Jesus elsewhere suggests that the religious person look where for ultimate and adequate commendation?

2 "One is your teacher . . . one is your master . . . one is your father": who is the one who was teacher, master, and father for Jesus?

3 "Whosoever shall exalt himself shall be humbled; and whosoever shall humble himself shall be exalted": what is the most complete act of self-humility that is within the range of human choice?

4 "He that is greatest among you shall be your minister": as against being what naturally and usually?

5 Of those religious attitudes, beliefs, and practices which called forth the woes pronounced by Jesus, what ones are observable in the religious leadership and life of our own day?

6 Why did Jesus reserve his most severe denunciation of contemporary religious leadership until he had reached Jerusalem?

7 Is Jesus to be commended or is he to be condemned for such devastating and biting criticism of the religious leaders?

8 "Fill ye up then the measure of your fathers": what was the outcome of that bold challenge?

9 "Laying wait for him, to catch something out of his mouth": since they had just heard much, very much, to which they would strenuously object and which was calculated to arouse violent opposition, what was the special nature of that which they hoped yet to hear?

§97 *The True Test of Giving*

"Of their superfluity" as over against "of her want": how formulate the norm for giving that finds expression in this narrative?

CHAPTER XVII

DISCOURSE ON EVENTS OF THE FUTURE

§98 *Discourse on Events of the Future*

1 "There shall not be left here one stone upon another": how many decades passed, subsequent to this forecast, before the siege of Jerusalem and the complete destruction of the temple by the Romans?

2 "Tell us *when* . . . what shall be the sign *when?*": so that the central theme of the discourse has to do with what element? b) So that the development of the discourse will have to do with events in so far only as they bear upon what?

3 "But the end is not yet": what end is meant here?

4 "The abomination of desolation": why the choice of this vague and cryptic form of designation to cover the Roman army and its equipment within the temple area?

5 "For those days shall be tribulation such as there hath not been the like from the beginning of the creation which God created until now and never shall be": to what historian may one go for the confirmatory details of the siege and destruction of Jerusalem by the Romans? b) On what recognized historical and contemporary facts was this forecast based in advance of its realization?

6 "This generation shall not pass away, until all these things be accomplished": what was the degree of accuracy in that time forecast relative to the destruction of Jerusalem?

7 "The days will come, when ye shall desire to see the Day of the Son of man": what are the circumstances in mind which it is asserted will create eagerness to see intervention by the apocalyptic representative of God?

8 "And ye shall not see it": how explain that tenacity of the human mind which nevertheless continues to modern times in eager expectation of apocalyptic manifestation?

9 "Many shall come, saying, I am the Christ; and, The time is at hand": what Jewish historian records vividly the succession of futile messianic political uprisings between the time of Jesus and the destruction of Jerusalem?

10 What single feature in the nature of the Day of the Son

of man is that which is most vividly and certainly conveyed by the poetic description which is here credited to Jesus? b) What bearing does that feature have upon the question of the *time* of the coming of that Day?

11 "Where the carcase is, thither will the vultures also be gathered together": how express otherwise the thought that is hidden in this cryptic and subtle response to the question of *Where* that lay behind *When*?

12 "But of that Day knoweth no one . . . Ye know not when the time is": while it is affirmed here that it is not possible for anybody but God to know the time of the Day of the Son of man, which event the disciples were destined so ardently to desire, Jesus is credited with fashioning the forecast that what decisive event would fall within the generation to which his message was addressed?

13 Apparently bearing within its structure some message relative to that *time* element which was so major and eager a concern of the disciples, the parable of the ten virgins has found a place within this discourse on the future: what was it that really distinguished the five wise virgins from the five foolish virgins?

14 "They all slumbered and slept": that recorded fact excludes the supposition that the difference between the wise and the foolish consisted in what attitude that is often attributed to the wise as against the foolish?

15 Since it cannot be asserted that the wise watched while the foolish went to sleep, what was it that ultimately differentiated the wise from the foolish? b) What bearing does that differentiation have upon the question of the *time* of events?

16 The wise virgins were prepared for what contingency that had not been taken into account by the foolish virgins? b) So that the suggestion of the parable is what about the *time* element?

17 What is the major element that dominates the thought throughout the statements about the mission of the disciples in the future?

18 "It shall turn unto you for a testimony": what other ways of thinking about persecution are more common than this interpretation?

19 "For it is not ye that speak, but the Spirit of your

Father that speaketh in you": in order for that to be true, what must be the fundamental attitude of the speaker toward God?

20 "And ye shall be hated of all men": what were the bases of the hatred created by the disciples of Jesus?

21 "Be ye therefore wise as serpents, and harmless as doves": in his own chosen policy throughout his teaching, wherein had Jesus shown himself to be as wise as a serpent?

22 "If they have called the master of the house Beelzebub": on what occasion was this charge levelled against Jesus, and with what outcome?

23 "There is nothing covered up, that shall not be revealed: and hid, that shall not be known": on what highly significant occasion had Jesus taught in a manner which he himself is reputed to have defined as calculated temporarily to cover up and to hide the truth that was being expounded?

24 "Speak ye in the light: proclaim upon the housetops. And I say unto you my friends, Be not afraid of them which kill the body, and after that have no more that they can do": in what period of the teaching of Jesus is it most eminently true that he personally followed the counsel here given to his disciples?

25 "He that heareth you heareth me; and he that rejecteth you rejecteth me; and he that rejecteth me rejecteth him that sent me": for these words to be anything other than an unsupported and arbitrary statement, what must be true about the nature of the fundamental attitude of Jesus and of his disciple toward God?

26 "To each according to his several ability . . . To whomsoever much is given, of him shall much be required": from whom is nothing whatever expected toward the advancement of the kingdom of God?

§99 *Teaching by Jesus in Jerusalem*

"And all the people came early in the morning to him in the temple, to hear him": indicative of the fact that the major interest of Jesus during the latter days of his life continued to be what form of activity? b) And with what response?

CHAPTER XVIII

FINAL HOURS OF JESUS WITH HIS DISCIPLES

§100 *Conspiracy for the Arrest of Jesus*

1 "Sought how they might take Jesus with subtilty": what were some of the methods already used which had proved futile? b) Why did those methods fail?

2 "Lest haply there shall be a tumult of the people" . . . "in the absence of the multitude": effective protection of Jesus during these final days, despite his outspoken arraignment of the religious leaders, rested on what major fact of the situation?

§101 *The Passover with the Disciples*

1 "With desire I have desired to eat this passover with you": how account for the fact that, though apparently this had been the original intention, Jesus did not himself actually participate in the passover when the time came?

2 "I will not eat" . . . "I will not drink": what caused the state of mind that brought about this attitude toward participation with the disciples?

3 "Until that day when I drink it new in the kingdom of God": what is the meaning and the significance of the term "new" in this saying?

4 What conception of the kingdom of God apparently stands behind the reputed references to it on this occasion?

§102 *Withdrawal to the Mount of Olives*

"Although all shall be offended, yet will not I" . . . "If I must die with thee, I will not deny thee": how account for the difference between this brave profession and the subsequent action of the man?

§103 *At the Place Named Gethsemane*

1 "Not what I will, but what thou wilt" . . . "Thy will be done": since Jesus clearly had no purpose to do anything

other than what he believed to be the will of God, what was the problem with which he was confronted in Gethsemane?

2 What were the alternatives that were open to Jesus, that is, what could he have done other than to accept arrest and death? b) Why did he hesitate to adopt one or other of these possible alternatives?

3 What evidence is there here that Jesus believed in the possibility of some divine intervention on his behalf?

4 "All things are possible unto thee": what position taken by Jesus throughout his life makes it difficult to believe that among the possibilities in the mind of Jesus was that of divine intervention in supernatural form?

5 "Remove this cup from me": what was the only way by which the cup could be removed from Jesus?

6 To what conclusion did Jesus come as a result of his prolonged prayer? b) What may have been some of the factors determining his final attitude?

§104 *Betrayal and Arrest of Jesus*

1 "Take him, and lead him away safely": wherein lay the danger against which they were determined to guard?

2 "All they that take the sword shall perish with the sword": what is the verdict of history as to the soundness or otherwise of that saying?

3 "When I was daily with you in the temple, ye stretched not forth your hands against me": why did the religious leaders hesitate to act under those circumstances?

4 "This is your hour, and the power of darkness": what have the centuries since thought about that judgment?

CHAPTER XIX

JUDICIAL TRIALS AND CRUCIFIXION OF JESUS

§105 *The Trial Before the Jewish Authorities*

1 "This man also was with Jesus" . . . "Thou also art one of them" . . . "Of a truth this man also was with Jesus: for he is a Galilaean": what did these observations portend that should lead Peter flatly to deny them?

2 "We heard him say, I will destroy this temple that is made with hands, and in three days I will build another made without hands": what had Jesus actually stated about the destruction of the temple? b) In the mind of Jesus, who were destined to be the destroyers? c) What basis can be found in the teaching of Jesus for some conception that would lend itself to the distortion that he would build another temple made without hands?

3 "What is it which these witness against thee?": what may be properly thought of that as the central question of the chief prosecutor?

4 "If thou art the Christ, tell us": what advantage would it be to the prosecution to possess some specific and definitely affirmative declaration on that point? b) What practical use could they make of such an affirmation that would contribute to the achievement of their purpose?

5 "If I tell you, ye will not believe": what stood in the way of their believing that Jesus was the Christ? b) Why would a statement that he was not the Christ have been unacceptable to them?

6 "If I ask you, ye will not answer": why should one ask questions as a part of the process of answering a question which by its nature seems to call for simply an affirmative or negative word?

7 "Art thou the Son of God?": judging from the content of this title in many preceding contexts, it may perhaps be regarded as the equivalent of what other more frequently used designation?

8 "Ye say that I am": what extended paraphrase of that final response by Jesus will convey its intended meaning?

§106 *The Trial Before the Roman Authorities*

1 "We found this man perverting our nation": if they had been called upon by the Roman governor to enumerate the specific points of perversion, what features of the teaching and actions of Jesus could have been advanced in support of their contention?

2 "We found this man forbidding to give tribute to Caesar": what had Jesus actually taught about the acute problem of Roman taxes?

3 "We found this man saying that he himself is Christ a king": on what occasions had Jesus ever declared that he believed himself to be the Messiah of the Jewish people? b) Or heard that designation from the lips of others without vigorous protest?

4 "Jesus answered Pilate and said, Thou sayest": which means an affirmative? or a negative? or is non-committal? or what?

5 "Jesus no more answered anything": how explain this attitude on the part of Jesus before both the Jewish and the Roman authorities?

6 "Pilate said unto the chief priests, I find no fault in this man": what would have been the attitude of Pilate toward Jesus if it were true that Jesus had claimed, in the presence of Pilate, and in response to his question, that he was the King of the Jews?

7 "He stirreth up the people, teaching throughout all Judaea, and beginning from Galilee even unto this place": in what sense did the Jewish authorities intend that Pilate should understand their charge that Jesus stirred up the people? b) Stirred up the people to what that would be of any concern to the Roman governor? c) Actually so far as Jesus had stirred the people it had been by teaching relative to issues of what nature?

8 "And he questioned him in many words; but Jesus answered him nothing": how account for this attitude on the part of Jesus toward Herod, tetrarch of Galilee?

9 "Having examined him before you, I found no fault in this man touching those things whereof ye accuse him: no, nor yet Herod": what were the areas of inquiry into the teaching of Jesus that would hold interest and concern for these two Roman rulers over the Jewish people? b) What

does the verdict of Pilate and Herod testify as to the relation of Jesus to the office of the Christ?

10 "I will therefore chastise him and release him": what was the motive of Pilate in offering to chastise a prisoner whom he had declared to be innocent of the charges brought against him?

11 "There was one called Barabbas, a notable prisoner, lying bound in prison with them that had made insurrection": since Barabbas was obviously notable among theocratic revolutionists against the rule of Rome, and Jesus openly an exponent of rendering unto Caesar the things that were Caesar's and unto God the things that were God's, for which of the two could the general multitude naturally be most effectually swayed by the chief priests and rulers?

12 "What then shall I do unto him whom ye call the King of the Jews?": what does the action of Pilate indicate as to his attitude toward this designation of Jesus by the chief priests and rulers who sought thus to have him destroyed?

§107 *The Crucifixion of Jesus*

1 "For behold, the days are coming": to what fate for Jerusalem and for the Jewish people does Jesus here make reference? b) What degree of soundness does history report as belonging to this forecast?

2 "For if they do these things in the green tree, what shall be done in the dry?": what was the underlying and essential nature of that which they were doing? b) In what way did that have any bearing in bringing about the future that Jesus foresaw?

3 "And Jesus said, Father, forgive them; for they know not what they do": what relation does this attitude of Jesus bear to the teaching Jesus had given throughout his life?

4 "He trusteth on God; let him deliver him now, if he desireth him": on what occasions during his lifetime had Jesus negatived the supposition that acceptability with God involved the assumption of intervention by God on behalf of the accepted person?

5 "And when the centurion, which stood by over against Jesus, saw what was done, he said, Certainly this was a righteous man": what have been the verdicts of the centuries since as to this contemporary judgment by a Roman soldier?

BOOK II

THE RECORD OF JOHN

PHILOSOPHY AND PSYCHOLOGY OF RELIGION

BOOK II

THE RECORD OF JOHN

PHILOSOPHY AND PSYCHOLOGY OF RELIGION

BOOK II
THE RECORD OF JOHN

PHILOSOPHY AND PSYCHOLOGY OF RELIGION

§1 *Prologue to the Record of John*

1 "In the beginning was the Word" . . . "The Word became flesh": of these two statements, which may be regarded as the distinctive contribution of the author of the record of John?

2 "As many as received him, to them gave he the right to become children of God, which were begotten, not of blood, nor of the will of the flesh, nor of the will of man, but of God": what is meant by "not of blood"? b) What is meant by "nor of the will of the flesh"? c) What is meant by "nor of the will of man"?

3 "The right to become children of God": what does this assume as to man's natural status as man before God?
b) Relationship to God is regarded as birthright? or achievement? Which?

4 "Which were begotten of God": by virtue of what on the part of man?

5 "For the law was given by Moses; grace and truth came through Jesus Christ": "the law" *versus* "grace and truth" as methods for the attainment of righteous and abundant life: what was that something which Jesus practised and taught as over against "the law"?

6 Wherein consists the ultimate futility of "the law" when considered as a discipline fashioned for the moral integration of the individual life?

7 What is the essential nature of that which must be substituted for "the law", if there is to be achieved at the same time complete order and complete freedom?

§2 *With a Jewish Teacher*

1 "Except a man be born anew" . . . "Except a man be born of the Spirit": what control does the individual have

over the process of being born of the flesh? b) What control does the individual have over the process of being born of the Spirit?

2 "Ye must be born anew": wherein would consist the validity of the injunction, if it be assumed that the individual is not the ultimately determinative factor in the production of the outcome?

3 What condition must the individual fulfil in order to be born anew?

4 "How can these things be?": what justification can be advanced for the use of figurative language so strong as that which is employed in this reputed talk with Nicodemus?

§3 *With a Samaritan Woman*

1 "Whosoever drinketh of the water that I shall give him shall never thirst; but the water that I shall give him shall become in him a well of water springing up unto eternal life": what should be regarded as that which has been derivative from Jesus for which it can be justly claimed that it possesses the qualities attributed to it here?

2 "God is a Spirit: and they that worship him must worship in spirit and truth": what material sacraments have been completely rejected by some historically significant and religiously potent Christian groups as being wholly alien within any truly spiritual religion?

§4 *With the Disciples*

"My meat is to do the will of him that sent me, and to accomplish his work": accepting this statement as the basis, what are some of the most important and confident assertions that might be made about a) the fundamental thought and b) the personal character of Jesus?

§5 *On the Bread of Life*

1 "Jesus answered and said unto them, This is the work of God, that ye believe on him whom he hath sent . . . I am the bread of life: he that cometh to me shall not hunger. For I am come down from heaven, not to do mine own will, but the will of him that sent me": from which succession of arresting statements it seems to become apparent that whoever believes enough in Jesus to come to him with the object of gaining

whatever of values there are resident in him thereby learns something fundamental about the direction of the personal will of Jesus. a) Of what practical value is that discovery to the discoverer? b) How establish the fact of any bond of functional relationship between that which is discovered and the fulfilment of ultimate human aspiration ("hunger") and outreaching?

2 "I am the living bread: if any man eat of this bread, he shall live forever": if one were to venture to depersonalize this saying, it might take the form—"Jesus is the living bread: if any man eat of this bread, he shall live forever": what words as paraphrase could then be substituted for "eat of this bread" that would do full justice to the whole saying as reported?

3 "As the living Father sent me, and I live because of the Father; so he also shall live because of me": by virtue of what attitude on the part of Jesus toward God did he live because of God? b) In what sense therefore may it be affirmed that it is because of Jesus that life has come to others?

4 "Except ye eat my flesh and drink my blood, ye have not life in yourselves. He that eateth my flesh and drinketh my blood hath eternal life" . . . "Doth this cause you to stumble? It is the spirit that quickeneth; the flesh profiteth nothing": since the flesh profiteth nothing, these words about flesh and blood apparently may be taken simply as extraordinarily vivid and most searching modes of conveying an intimacy of relationship or likeness of the most fundamental kind between the teacher and the disciple: what is the single condition for the most complete alignment of the self with the ultimate spirit of Jesus?

§6 *On the Light of Life*

1 "He that followeth me shall not walk in the darkness": followeth Jesus toward what or whom? b) By what mode of functioning did Jesus mediate the light of life?

2 "I am he that beareth witness of myself, and the Father that sent me beareth witness of me": what is the medium through which it may be supposed Jesus thought God conveyed to man his estimate of Jesus?

3 "If ye were blind, ye would have no sin: but now ye say, We see: your sin remaineth": how describe broadly that human attitude of which this judgment is so severe an arraign-

ment? b) What is the only completely adequate destroyer of that attitude?

4 "Every one that doeth ill hateth the light, and cometh not to the light . . . But he that doeth the truth cometh to the light": in other words, that one apparently most in need of light turns away from light, and that one turns toward light who is not lacking in light: what is the real nature of the ultimate need of that one who turns away from light?

§7 *Several Sayings of Jesus*

1 "And cometh not into judgement": as opposed to what different conception about what the future held?

2 "Hath passed out of death into life": what is the distinctive element in this thought?

3 "Except the Father draw him": what is the medium and what the mode of the activity of the Father relative to Jesus? b) In what measure is the action of God arbitrary?

4 "My judgement is righteous, because I seek not mine own will, but the will of him that sent me": what is the explanation of the fact that soundness in the direction of the will profoundly affects every area of the functioning of the personality?

5 "Because ye think that in them ye have eternal life": what are some of the other prominent supposed bases of eternal life that stand outside the boundaries of the way of life as enunciated by Jesus?

6 "For I do always the things that are pleasing to him": how should one account for the fact that this form of loyalty makes man independent of man?

7 "Before Abraham was, I am": how old is the will of God? b) What was the relation that Jesus bore to the will of God?

§8 *On Freedom through Truth*

1 "If ye abide in my word, then are ye truly my disciples": what are some of the much more customary conditions set forth by tradition as the essentials of discipleship to Jesus?

2 "If ye abide in my word, ye shall know the truth": the word of Jesus was wholly concerned with the truth about what that is significant to man?

3 "The truth shall make you free": truth about what shall

make one free? b) Shall make one free from what? c) What is the most ultimate of all bondages?

4 "Every one that committeth sin is the bondservant of sin": what is the specified method of Jesus for the achievement of such freedom as is to be had from this bondage?

§9 *On Life through Loyalty*

1 "I know him, and keep his word": in the case of Jesus, what did it mean on his part to keep the word of God?

2 "If a man keep my word, he shall never see death": what was the ultimate and determinative word of Jesus?

§10 *On Jesus as Son*

1 "Called God his own Father, making himself equal with God": what measure of justification was there for drawing this deduction from the mode of reference to God used by Jesus?

2 "Because that thou, being a man, makest thyself God": what content may reasonably be given to the declaration "I and the Father are one" that does not carry within it the implication that Jesus was thereby making himself God?

3 "The Father is in me, and I in the Father": was that profound relationship fortuitous? or God-determined? or determined by Jesus? b) What was the mode of its achievement?

§11 *Several Sayings of Jesus*

1 "He that believeth on me" . . . "whosoever liveth and believeth on me": in view of the stupendous nature of the outcome, what content should be given here to the term "believeth"?

2 "That they may have life, and may have it abundantly": what justification is there for regarding the way to life as itself restrictive in nature and therefore making against the abundant life?

3 "This is life eternal: that they should know the only true God": what is the process set forth by Jesus for entering into that knowledge of God which has significance for the life of man?

4 "Except a grain of wheat fall into the earth and die, it abideth by itself alone; but if it die, it beareth much fruit": in the search to discover what this means in the realm of the human spirit, what content exactly should be given to the phrase

"fall into the earth and die", that is, what is the counterpart within personality of this process? b) What is the phase of personality that is primarily involved in this manner of ceasing to "abide by one's self alone"?

5 "He that loveth his life loseth it; and he that hateth his life shall keep it": what is intended to be covered by the term "life" in this saying?

6 "He that hateth his life": what is the motive here for doing that? b) Wherein does that motive differ from "loveth his life"?

7 "He that loveth his life": with what ultimate motive in mind? b) Whether is that motive to be commended or to be condemned?

8 "He that loveth his life loseth it; and he that hateth his life shall keep it": since the motive in both halves of the saying is the same, and in neither half is criticized, wherein does the element that is regarded unfavorably consist?

9 "He that loveth his life loseth it; and he that hateth his life shall keep it": what are the two most crucial words in this saying? b) What precisely does each of them mean?

10 "Loseth it" . . . "shall keep it": what does each of these alternative outcomes really mean as ultimate resultants?

§12 *Source of the Teaching*

1 "If any man hear my sayings, and keep them not" . . . "He that receiveth not my sayings": what evaluation is here placed upon the teaching function in the life of Jesus?

2 "The word that I spake, the same shall judge him": if that be so, what place should be given to the study of the teaching of Jesus?

3 "And I know that his commandment is life eternal": by what process may others than Jesus come to the same conviction?

4 "The things therefore which I speak, even as the Father hath said unto me, so I speak": by what manner of test may one determine whether this statement is a) mere confident assertion or b) demonstrable truth?

§13 *Test for the Teaching*

1 "How knoweth this man letters, having never learned?": in what degree is fundamental religious insight the product

of intellectual discipline? b) Of what primarily is that insight the resultant?

2 "If any man willeth to do his will, he shall know of the teaching, whether it be of God, or whether I speak from myself": knowledge of the ultimate truth about religion becomes, under this mode of test, the product of the functioning of what element in personality? b) What place does the intellect have in arriving at elemental truth in the area of religion?

§14 *Estimate of the Teaching*

"Never man so spake": of what other teacher can it be affirmed that he not only taught what he believed to be the truth but that he also enunciated clearly that method for the testing of the truth of what he taught which is universally available?

§15 *Farewell Discourse of Jesus*

1 "I am the way, and the truth, and the life": in what sense precisely may it be affirmed that Jesus is the way? b) wherein consists the legitimacy in saying that Jesus is the truth? c) to what must one go back if one asserts that Jesus is the life?

2 "No one cometh unto the Father but by me": with what meaning must "by me" be taken, if this assertion is to be regarded as verified by history?

3 "He that hath seen me hath seen the Father": how refashion that statement so as to make it more easily intelligible and convincing?

4 "Believe me that I am in the Father, and the Father in me": in what source did that sense of unity originate?

5 "Abide in me, and I in you" . . . "He that abideth in me, and I in him": from this mode of expressing the essential relationship between the disciple and Jesus, what can be learned as to the intended meaning in the statement "I am in the Father, and the Father in me" when used to describe the essential relationship between Jesus and God?

6 "When the Spirit of truth is come, which proceedeth from the Father, he shall bear witness of me": what is the nature and the content of that attestation given by the Spirit of truth relative to Jesus?

7 "In that day ye shall know that I am in my Father, and

ye in me, and I in you": what is the fundamental basis, or the underlying condition, for that sense of unity between the disciple and Jesus and between Jesus and God which is here affirmed as open to experience?

8 "If a man love me, he will keep my word: and my Father will love him, and we will come unto him, and make our abode with him": the sense of the abiding inward presence of God is here made dependent upon what attitude toward what?

b) What is the ultimate and determinative "word" of Jesus that he would have kept?

9 "This is my commandment, that ye love one another" . . . "A new commandment I give unto you, that ye love one another" . . . "By this shall all men know that ye are my disciples, if ye have love one to another": whether is the attitude here commended by Jesus a) a way toward the achievement of freedom and life, or b) an expression of freedom and life already otherwise achieved?

10 "The Father shall give you another, that he may be with you for ever, even the Spirit of truth" . . . "Howbeit when he, the Spirit of truth, is come, he shall guide you into all the truth" . . . "The Holy Spirit, whom the Father will send, he shall teach you all things": what is the ultimate ground for believing, apart from the affirmative assertion of anybody, that the truly religious person, as defined in the terms of Jesus, may become the possessor of significant intellectual insights not granted to others?

11 "The Father is greater than I": elsewhere Jesus is credited with saying "I and the Father are one": in what sense must the latter phrase be taken, in order for the former phrase and the latter phrase to be both harmonious and fully intelligible?

12 "As the Father gave me commandment, even so I do": what is the relation between this personal attitude on the part of Jesus and that which Jesus elsewhere sets forth as the sole condition for one's becoming a truly religious person?

§16 *Farewell Prayer of Jesus*

1 "The work which thou hast given me to do . . . the words which thou gavest me I have given unto them" . . . "They have kept thy word": from which it may be deduced

that Jesus considered his sole function as consisting in what form of activity?

2 "All things that are mine are thine, and thine are mine": in what measure is the degree of truth in the second phrase dependent upon the reality of the attitude expressed in the initial phrase?

3 "I have given them thy word" . . . "Sanctify them in the truth: thy word is truth": from which it is to be understood that the teaching activity of Jesus was regarded as possessing what significance?

4 "That they may be one, even as we are" . . . "that they may all be one; even as thou, Father, art in me, and I in thee, that they also may be in us" . . . "that they may be one, even as we are one; I in them, and thou in me, that they may be perfected into one": what is the single fundamental condition, enunciated clearly and repeatedly elsewhere by Jesus, that must be fulfilled in order for the achievement of that which makes of God, of Jesus, and of the disciples of Jesus, one single interpenetrating unity—God in Jesus, God in the disciples, Jesus in God, Jesus in the disciples, the disciples in Jesus, the disciples in God?

§17 *Jesus and Pilate*

1 "To this end have I been born, and to this end am I come into the world, that I should bear witness unto the truth": what relation does this formulation of the function and purpose of Jesus bear to that which is most generally regarded as the intention and meaning of his life?

2 "To this end have I been born, and to this end am I come into the world, that I should bear witness unto the truth": what is that central truth about the nature of mature religion to which Jesus bore witness in word consistently throughout his life?